ASVAB

CALCULATION WORKBOOK

ISBN: 1734820373
ISBN-13: 978-1734820379

CONTENTS

PART 1

ARITHMETIC REASONING

PRACTICE TEST 1

QUESTIONS

1. Sarah purchased a new home with an initial down payment of $80,000. If she has a 30-year mortgage which requires a monthly payment of $1,200, then how much will Sarah pay in total for the home?

   A. $490,000
   B. $498,000
   C. $504,000
   D. $512,000

2. A food truck sold eight hamburgers for $6.99 each, six hot dogs for $4.99 each, and 14 drinks for $1.99 each. If the total cost of food and labor was $75, then how much profit did the food truck earn?

   A. $29.17
   B. $38.72
   C. $45.68
   D. $53.24

3. Ben's grade for math class is comprised of six quizzes and one final exam. If each quiz makes up $\frac{1}{9}$ of the final grade, then what percent of Ben's grade is based on the final exam?

   A. 25%
   B. 30%
   C. 33%
   D. 36%

4. If the ratio of people with blonde hair to brown hair in a particular group is 5:7, then which of the following could be the total number of people in the group?

   A. 128
   B. 136
   C. 144
   D. 152

5. If a salesman left the office for a sales call at 9:00 a.m. and returned at 4:30 p.m., how long was he out of the office?

   A. 27,000 seconds
   B. 28,000 seconds
   C. 29,000 seconds
   D. 30,000 seconds

6. A landscaping company is planting a circular flower garden. If the garden is 18 feet in diameter, then what is its approximate area?

   A. 241.65 square feet
   B. 254.34 square feet
   C. 263.70 square feet
   D. 278.19 square feet

7. Candace, Adam, and John are house painters. At their latest job, Candace painted 36% of the house and Adam painted $\frac{1}{4}$ of the house. What percentage of the house did John paint?

   A. 33%
   B. 35%
   C. 38%
   D. 39%

8. A construction crew is installing a concrete tennis court at a local park. The dimensions of the tennis court will be 80 feet by 9 yards, and the concrete will be 6 inches thick. If the cost of concrete is $100 per cubic yard, then what volume of concrete will be needed to complete the project?

   A. 1,004 cubic feet
   B. 1,080 cubic feet
   C. 1,126 cubic feet
   D. 1,194 cubic feet

9. Train A and Train B each left the station at 12 p.m. Train A was headed east toward Atlanta, and Train B was headed west toward Memphis. If Train A traveled at 45 miles per hour, and Train B traveled at 60 miles per hour, then how far apart were the trains at the end of 2 hours?

   A. 180 miles
   B. 190 miles
   C. 210 miles
   D. 240 miles

10. Mary Beth, an architect, is redesigning an office building and trying to maximize the size of the square-shaped lobby. If she were to increase the length of the lobby by 20%, by what percent would its area increase?

   A. 20%
   B. 40%
   C. 44%
   D. 50%

11. If David's monthly salary decreases from $4,800 to $4,200, the percentage change is:

    A. –12.5%
    B. –9.8%
    C. –6.2%
    D. –5.5%

12. An artist is painting a mural that measures 15 feet by 8 feet. What is the area of the mural?

    A. 96 square feet
    B. 120 square feet
    C. 240 square feet
    D. 289 square feet

13. 17 red marbles and three times as many blue marbles add up to one-fourth the number of green marbles. How many green marbles are there?

    A. 156
    B. 174
    C. 218
    D. 272

14. Frank took a 6-hour flight from Miami to Los Angeles. If he left Miami at 10 a.m. and there is a three hour time difference between the two cities, then what time did Frank arrive in Los Angeles?

    A. 10 a.m.
    B. 1 p.m.
    C. 4 p.m.
    D. 7 p.m.

15. If 22,000 people attended a football game, which was 10% more than the stadium operator had anticipated, then how many people were expected to attend?

    A. 19,800
    B. 20,000
    C. 21,500
    D. 24,200

16. If a photographer can take pictures of 6 clients per day, then how many clients can he serve if he works every day for the months of August and September?

    A. 366
    B. 382
    C. 394
    D. 400

17. Tommy was paid $35 for 5 hours of yard work. His friend, Jimmy, received $50 for 6 hours of yard work. How much higher was Jimmy's hourly wage than Tommy's?

    A. $0.67
    B. $1.00
    C. $1.33
    D. $1.67

18. If a race track is 1.25 miles long, then how many miles is 35 laps?

    A. 35.25
    B. 38.50
    C. 40.25
    D. 43.75

19. Jen bought five cartons of eggs on sale. A single carton normally costs $2.50, but she was able to purchase five cartons for a total cost of $10.00. How much money did Jen save on her purchase?

    A. $2.50
    B. $3.00
    C. $3.50
    D. $4.00

20. In five consecutive basketball games, a player scored the following number points: 25, 24, 28, 25, and 18. What is the mode of these point totals?

    A. 24
    B. 25
    C. 26
    D. 28

21. Luke has a savings account that pays an annual interest rate of 6%. What are the equivalent monthly and quarterly interest rates?

    A. 0.5% monthly interest rate, 1.5% quarterly interest rate
    B. 1.5% monthly interest rate, 0.5% quarterly interest rate
    C. 4.5% monthly interest rate, 6.0% quarterly interest rate
    D. 48% monthly interest rate, 24% quarterly interest rate

22. A rancher needs 20 sections of rope, each 12 feet 4 inches long, to secure livestock. If rope is sold by the foot, then what is the minimum length the rancher must buy?

    A. 243 feet
    B. 245 feet
    C. 247 feet
    D. 249 feet

23. The dimensions of a park are 300 feet by 200 feet. If the park includes a square pavilion measuring 35 feet on each side, then what is the area of the park not covered by the pavilion?

   A. 1,226 square feet
   B. 58,775 square feet
   C. 60,000 square feet
   D. 61,225 square feet

24. Tony is on a diet and monitoring his calories this week. Sunday through Friday, Tony averaged 2,100 calories per day. If he consumes 1,900 calories on Saturday, then what will be his average daily calories consumed for the week?

   A. 1,986
   B. 2,004
   C. 2,045
   D. 2,071

25. An art dealer bought a painting for $6,000 and sold it the following week for $6,600. What was the percent profit on the sale?

   A. 7%
   B. 8%
   C. 9%
   D. 10%

ANSWER KEY

1. D
Step 1: Calculate the length of the mortgage.
30 years × 12 months per year = 360 months

Step 2: Calculate the total monthly payments.
360 months × $1,200 per month = $432,000

Step 3: Find the total cost.
$432,000 + $80,000 = $512,000

2. B
Hamburger sales: 8 × $6.99 = $55.92
Hot dog sales: 6 × $4.99 = $29.94
Drink sales: 14 × $1.99 = $27.86
Total sales: $55.92 + $29.94 + $27.86 = $113.72
Profit: $113.72 – $75.00 = $38.72

3. C
If each quiz makes represents $\frac{1}{9}$ of the final grade, and there are six quizzes, then the quizzes make up $\frac{6}{9}$ of the final grade. That leaves $\frac{3}{9}$ remaining for the final exam, which can be expressed as $\frac{1}{3}$ or 33%.

4. C
If the ratio is 5:7 then there are 12 parts in the ratio. Therefore, the total number of people in the group must be a multiple of 12. The only choice listed that is a multiple of 12 is 144. In this question, the ratio would be 60:84, which can be reduced to 5:7.

5. A
There are 7.5 hours between 9:00 a.m. and 4:30 p.m.
7.5 hours × 60 minutes per hour × 60 seconds per minute = 27,000 seconds

6. B
Area = π × radius²
Area = 3.14 × (9 feet)² =
Area = 3.14 × 81 square feet = 254.34 square feet

7. D
Percent painted by Candace: 36%, which can be expressed as $\frac{36}{100}$.
Percent painted by Adam: $\frac{1}{4}$, which can be expressed as $\frac{25}{100}$.
Percent painted by Candace and Adam: $\frac{36}{100} + \frac{25}{100} = \frac{61}{100}$, which can be expressed as 61%.
Percent painted by John: 100% – 61% = 39%

8. B
Step 1: Convert yards to feet. 9 yards × 3 feet per yard = 27 feet
Step 2: Convert inches to feet. 6 inches ÷ 12 inches per foot = 0.5 feet
Step 3: Calculate the volume. 80 feet × 27 feet × 0.5 feet = 1,080 cubic feet

9. C
Step 1: Calculate distance traveled for Train A. 45 miles per hour × 2 hours = 90 miles
Step 2: Calculate distance traveled for Train B. 60 miles per hour × 2 hours = 120 miles
Step 3: Find the total distance traveled. 90 miles + 120 miles = 210 miles

10. C
Step 1: Substitute a number, such as 10, for the length of each side of the square lobby and solve. Because 20% of 10 is 2, the new length of each side would be 10 + 2 = 12.
Step 2: Calculate the area of the square with the new dimensions. 12 × 12 = 144
Step 3: Calculate the area of the square with the original dimensions. 10 × 10 = 100
Step 4: Calculate the percent increase. $\frac{(144 - 100)}{100} = \frac{44}{100} = 0.44 = 44\%$

11. A
Percent change = (new salary – old salary) ÷ old salary
Percent change = ($4,200 – $4,800) ÷ $4,800
Percent change = –$600 ÷ $4,800 = –0.125 = –12.5%

12. B
Area = length × width
Area = 15 feet × 8 feet = 120 square feet

13. D
Let g equal the number of green marbles.
17 + (17 × 3) = (0.25)g
17 + 51 = 0.25g
68 = 0.25g
272 = g

14. B
If the flight was 6 hours and Frank left at 10 a.m., then he arrived at 4 p.m. After adjusting for the time difference between the Eastern and Pacific time zones, the local time in Los Angeles was three hours earlier, or 1 p.m.

15. B
The actual attendance was 10% more than expected, which can be expressed as $\frac{11}{10}$ or 1.1. Next, solve for the expected attendance by using the equation 1.1x = 22,000. Solve for x by dividing both sides of the equation by 1.1. Therefore x = 20,000.

16. A
Step 1: Find the number of days in the months of August and September.
31 days (August) + 30 days (September) = 61 days

Step 2: Calculate the number of clients served.
61 days × 6 clients per day = 366 clients

17. C
Step 1: Calculate Tommy's hourly wage. $35 ÷ 5 hours = $7.00 per hour
Step 2: Calculate Jimmy's hourly wage. $50 ÷ 6 hours = $8.33 per hour
Step 3: Find the difference in wages. $8.33 – $7.00 = $1.33

18. D

35 laps × 1.25 miles per lap = 43.75 miles

19. A

Step 1: Calculate the cost of 5 cartons at full price. $2.50 per carton × 5 cartons = $12.50
Step 2: Find the difference between the sale price and full price. $12.50 – $10.00 = $2.50

20. B

25 is the only number that appears twice, therefore it is the mode.

21. A

Monthly interest rate = 6% per year ÷ 12 months per year = 0.5%
Quarterly interest rate = 6% per year ÷ 4 quarters per year = 1.5%

22. C

Step 1: Calculate the length of rope needed for each section, in inches.
12 feet × 12 inches per foot = 144 inches
144 inches + 4 inches = 148 inches

Step 2: Calculate the total length of rope needed for all sections, in inches.
20 sections × 148 inches per section = 2,960 inches

Step 3: Calculate the amount of rope needed, in feet.
2,960 inches ÷ 12 inches per foot = 246.67 feet (Round up to 247 feet.)

23. B

Step 1: Calculate the area of the park.
300 feet × 200 feet = 60,000 square feet

Step 2: Calculate the area of the pavilion.
35 feet × 35 feet = 1,225 square feet

Step 3: Find the area not covered by the pavilion.
60,000 square feet – 1,225 square feet = 58,775 square feet

24. D

Step 1: Calculate the total calories consumed for the first 6 days.
2,100 calories per day × 6 days = 12,600 calories

Step 2: Calculate the weekly average.
(12,600 calories + 1,900 calories) ÷ 7 days =
14,500 calories ÷ 7 days = 2,071 calories per day

25. D

Profit = (sale price – purchase price) ÷ purchase price
Profit = ($6,600 – $6,000) ÷ $6,000
Profit = $600 ÷ $6,000 = 0.1 = 10%

PRACTICE TEST 2

QUESTIONS

1. Phil's school is hosting a 10-mile walk-a-thon, and he received pledges of $18 per mile. Unfortunately, 8 miles into the walk-a-thon he sprained his ankle and had to stop walking. How much additional money could Phil have earned if he completed the entire 10 miles?

    A. $18
    B. $36
    C. $54
    D. $72

2. If a restaurant increases the price of an entrée from $30 to $33, by what percent did the price increase?

    A. 10%
    B. 11%
    C. 12%
    D. 13%

3. Linda loaned Kevin $400 with an annual interest rate of 7%. How much money will Kevin owe Linda after one year?

    A. $407
    B. $414
    C. $421
    D. $428

4. William and Carl are participating in a bike race. If William bikes at a rate of 18 miles per hour, and Carl bikes at a rate of 16 miles per hour, then how far apart will they be after 3.5 hours?

    A. 5 miles
    B. 7 miles
    C. 8 miles
    D. 10 miles

5. A baker prepared 12 cakes for a bake sale. However, 4 of the cakes were ruined during transit. If the ingredients for all 12 cakes cost $60, then how much will each of the remaining cakes have to sell for on average for the baker to earn twice the cost of the total ingredients?

    A. $10
    B. $12
    C. $15
    D. $18

6. According to the scale of a map, 1.5 inches is equal to 60 miles. If the distance between two cities is 2.5 inches, then how far apart are the cities?

    A. 100 miles
    B. 115 miles
    C. 120 miles
    D. 125 miles

7. Elizabeth's utility bills for the last four months were $212.87, $196.23, $189.15, and $206.96. What was the average monthly cost of the utilities?

    A. $200.20
    B. $201.30
    C. $204.10
    D. $207.80

8. A salesman typically drives 800 miles during his 45-hour work week. If he spends half his time in the car, how many hours does this equal?

    A. 19.5
    B. 20.0
    C. 21.0
    D. 22.5

9. If Speedy Mechanics charges $45 per hour, and Zippy Mechanics charges $40 per hour, what is the total difference in price if a job were to take 7.25 hours?

    A. $36.25
    B. $37.75
    C. $38.50
    D. $39.25

10. Three slices of pizza and a drink costs $5.80. One slice of pizza and a drink costs $2.60. How much would two slices of pizza and two drinks cost?

    A. $4.40
    B. $4.80
    C. $5.20
    D. $5.80

11. A farmer is installing a cylinder-shaped silo that is 20 feet in diameter and 45 feet high. What is the approximate volume of the silo?

    A. 13,670 cubic feet
    B. 14,130 cubic feet
    C. 15,310 cubic feet
    D. 16,240 cubic feet

12. A football coach would like to provide at least one pint of water to each of his players before practice. If the coach brings two large containers, each filed with 6 gallons of water, then how many pint-sized bottles can the coach fill?

    A. 78
    B. 84
    C. 90
    D. 96

13. Anna has a lemonade stand with 30 cups for sale. She sells one-third of the cups to her friends and half of the cups to neighbors. If she drinks one-sixth of the cups herself, then how many cups does Anna have left?

    A. 0
    B. 1
    C. 3
    D. 5

14. Christian drove 300 miles from Pittsburgh to Philadelphia. If his car gets 25 miles per gallon, and gas is $2.19 per gallon, then how much was the cost of gasoline for his trip?

    A. $24.94
    B. $25.46
    C. $26.28
    D. $27.12

15. A large group of friends is renting a basketball court for 2 hours. If there are 30 people who want to play, but only 10 people can be on the court at the same time, then how long can each person play?

    A. 30 minutes
    B. 40 minutes
    C. 50 minutes
    D. 60 minutes

16. A factory manufactures a product at a cost of 25 cents per unit, and each unit sells for 45 cents. If the factory has a monthly overhead cost of $5,000, then how many units of product must the factory sell each month to make a profit?

    A. 25,000
    B. 25,001
    C. 40,000
    D. 40,001

17. Lisa is three years younger than Mary. Carrie is five years older than Mary. The sum of all of their ages is 62. How old is Mary?

   A. 17 years old
   B. 19 years old
   C. 20 years old
   D. 22 years old

18. A four-digit code must be used to turn off a security alarm. If each of the four digits is a number between 0 and 9, then how many code combinations are possible?

   A. 900
   B. 1,000
   C. 9,000
   D. 10,000

19. Nina works for a zoo and needs to fill a rectangular aquarium with water. How much water will be added if the aquarium measures 3 feet by 2 yards by 6 inches?

   A. 9 cubic feet
   B. 18 cubic feet
   C. 27 cubic feet
   D. 36 cubic feet

20. Jordan would like to repave his driveway that is 18 feet wide, 50 feet long, and 3 inches thick. Concrete costs $100 per cubic yard and labor costs $5 per square foot. What is the cost of labor to repave the driveway?

   A. $4,300
   B. $4,400
   C. $4,500
   D. $4,600

21. A house was listed for sale for $200,000. If the seller accepted an offer that was 8% below the list price, then what was the final selling price?

   A. $176,000
   B. $178,000
   C. $182,000
   D. $184,000

22. A librarian is checking in a 4-foot high stack of returned library books. If each book is 1.5 inches thick, then how many books are in the stack?

   A. 32
   B. 34
   C. 35
   D. 36

23. If $\frac{3}{8}$ of a pizza has been eaten, then what is the ratio of the uneaten portion to the amount that has already been eaten?

    A. 4:3
    B. 5:3
    C. 6:2
    D. 8:3

24. Zach earns $15 per hour for his normal work shift from 9:00 a.m. to 5:00 p.m. He gets paid an extra $2 per hour for any overtime hours that he works. If Zack earned $171 for the day, then what time did he stop working?

    A. 8:00 p.m.
    B. 8:30 p.m.
    C. 9:30 p.m.
    D. 10:00 p.m.

25. A football team has a 0.2 probability of scoring a touchdown whenever they have possession of the football. If they have three attempts to score in the first quarter, then what is the probability that they will score a touchdown all three times?

    A. 0.004
    B. 0.008
    C. 0.010
    D. 0.012

ANSWER KEY

1. B
Step 1: Find the number of miles remaining. 10 miles – 8 miles = 2 miles
Step 2: Calculate the additional money earned. 2 miles × $18 per mile = $36

2. A
Percent change = (new price – old price) ÷ old price
Percent change = ($33 – $30) ÷ $30
Percent change = $3 ÷ $30 = 0.1 = 10%

3. D
Step 1: Calculate the annual interest. $400 × 0.07 = $28
Step 2: Find the loan balance after one year: $400 + $28 = $428
Alternatively, you could find the answer by $400 × 1.07 = $428.

4. B
Step 1: Calculate William's distance traveled. 18 miles per hour × 3.5 hours = 63 miles
Step 2: Calculate Carl's distance traveled. 16 miles per hour × 3.5 hours = 56 miles
Step 3: Find the difference in miles. 63 miles – 56 miles = 7 miles

5. C
For the baker to earn twice the cost of the ingredients, he will need to earn a total of $120. Because there were originally 12 cakes but 4 were ruined, there are only 8 cakes remaining for sale. Therefore, he will need to sell each cake for $15.
$120 ÷ 8 cakes = $15 per cake

6. A
If 1.5 inches equal 60 miles, cross multiply to find how many miles equals 2.5 inches.

$$\frac{1.5 \text{ inches}}{60 \text{ miles}} = \frac{2.5 \text{ inches}}{x \text{ miles}}$$

1.5x = 2.5 × 60
1.5x = 150
x = 100
The cities are 100 miles apart.

7. B
Average cost = ($212.87 + $196.23 + $189.15 + $206.96) ÷ 4
Average cost = $805.21 ÷ 4 = $201.30

8. D
45 hours × 0.5 = 22.5 hours

9. A
Step 1: Calculate Speedy Mechanics' price. $45 per hour × 7.25 hours = $326.25
Step 2: Calculate Zippy Mechanics' price. $40 per hour × 7.25 hours = $290.00
Step 3: Find the difference in price. $326.25 – $290.00 = $36.25

10. C
Step 1: Set up an equation where pizza = p and drink = d, and then solve for d.
3p + 1d = $5.80
d = $5.80 – 3p

Step 2: Find the cost of a slice of pizza.
1p + 1d = $2.60
1p + $5.80 – 3p = $2.60
–2p = –$3.20
p = $1.60

Step 3: Substitute the cost of a slice of pizza into the equation and solve for the cost of a drink.
1p + 1d = $2.60
1($1.60) + 1d = $2.60
$1.60 + 1d = $2.60
d = $1.00

Step 4: Find the cost of two slices of pizza and two drinks.
Cost = 2p + 2d
Cost = 2($1.60) + 2($1.00)
Cost = $3.20 + $2.00 = $5.20

11. B
Volume of a cylinder = π × radius² × height
Volume of a cylinder = 3.14 × (10 feet)² × 45 feet =
Volume of a cylinder = 3.14 × 100 square feet × 45 feet = 14,130 cubic feet

12. D
There are 8 pints in a gallon, therefore each 6-gallon water container can hold 48 pints. Because there are 2 containers, the coach can fill 96 bottles.

13. A
Find the lowest common denominator and convert each fraction. Then add them together.

$$\frac{1}{3} \times \frac{2}{2} = \frac{2}{6}$$

$$\frac{1}{2} \times \frac{3}{3} = \frac{3}{6}$$

$$\frac{2}{6} + \frac{3}{6} + \frac{1}{6} = \frac{6}{6} = 100\%$$

Anna has sold or consumed 30 cups of lemonade (100%) and has 0 cups left to sell.

14. C
Step 1: Calculate the number of gallons needed.
300 miles ÷ 25 miles per gallon = 12 gallons

Step 2: Calculate the total cost.
12 gallons × $2.19 per gallon = $26.28

15. B
Step 1: Divide the total number of people by the number who can play at the same time.
$30 \div 10 = 3$

Step 2: Calculate the amount of time each person can play.
(2 hours × 60 minutes per hour) ÷ 3 =
120 minutes ÷ 3 = 40 minutes

16. B
Step 1: Find the profit per unit.
$0.45 – $0.25 = $0.20

Step 2: Calculate the number of units needed to break even.
$5,000 ÷ $0.20 profit per unit = 25,000 units

If 25,000 units are needed to break even, then the factory must sell at least 25,001 units to make a profit.

17. C
Let Mary's age equal x. Therefore, Lisa's age is x – 3 and Carrie's age is x + 5.
$x + (x - 3) + (x + 5) = 62$
$x + x - 3 + x + 5 = 62$
$3x + 2 = 62$
$3x = 60$
$x = 20$
Mary is 20 years old.

18. D
There are 10 possibilities for each of the four digits of the code. (Remember to include "0" as a possibility.) The number of code combinations is $10 \times 10 \times 10 \times 10 = 10,000$. This can also be expressed as $10^4 = 10,000$.

19. A
Step 1: Convert yards to feet. 2 yards × 3 feet per yard = 6 feet
Step 2: Convert inches to feet. 6 inches ÷ 12 inches per foot = 0.5 feet
Step 3: Calculate the volume. 3 feet × 6 feet × 0.5 feet = 9 cubic feet

20. C
Step 1: Calculate the area of the driveway. 18 feet × 50 feet = 900 square feet
Step 2: Calculate the cost of labor = 900 square feet × $5 per square foot = $4,500

21. D
Step 1: Calculate the discount. $200,000 × 0.08 = $16,000
Step 2: Find the adjusted price. $200,000 – $16,000 = $184,000

22. A
Step 1: Calculate the height of the stack in inches. 4 feet × 12 inches per foot = 48 inches
Step 2: Calculate the number of books. 48 inches ÷ 1.5 inches per book = 32 books

23. B
If $\frac{3}{8}$ of the pizza has been eaten, then $\frac{5}{8}$ of the pizza remains. The ratio is 5:3.

24. A
Step 1: Calculate Zach's normal wage. 8 hours × $15 per hour = $120
Step 2: Find the amount of overtime pay. $171 – $120 = $51 overtime pay
Step 3: Find Zach's overtime wage per hour. $15 + $2 = $17
Step 4: Calculate the number of overtime hours worked. $51 ÷ $17 per hour = 3 hours
If Zach normally ends his shift at 5:00 p.m. but worked 3 extra hours, then his shift ended at 8:00 p.m.

25. B
The probability that all three possessions will result in a touchdown is 0.2 × 0.2 × 0.2 = 0.008.

PRACTICE TEST 3

QUESTIONS

1. Last week Steve mowed six lawns. His earnings, including tips, were as follows: $36, $40, $22, $33, $27, and $42. If Steve spent 30% of his earnings on gas and supplies, then how much money did he spend?

   A. $40
   B. $50
   C. $60
   D. $70

2. If Kate traveled 220 miles from Boston to New York City in 4 hours, then how fast did she travel?

   A. 40 miles per hour
   B. 45 miles per hour
   C. 50 miles per hour
   D. 55 miles per hour

3. A crew is hired to paint a large triangular portion of a building's interior. If the width of the triangle is 50 feet and the height is 25 feet, then what is the area of the space that will be painted?

   A. 525 square feet
   B. 550 square feet
   C. 625 square feet
   D. 700 square feet

4. Rob, a carpenter, charges a $50 fee to show up to a job site, and then an additional $45 per hour that he works. Yesterday, he arrived at a job site at 9 a.m. and charged $230 for the day. What time did Rob finish working?

   A. 12 p.m.
   B. 1 p.m.
   C. 2 p.m.
   D. 3 p.m.

5. Angela loaned money to a friend and charged an interest rate of 1.5% per month. What is the equivalent annual interest rate?

   A. 6%
   B. 9%
   C. 16%
   D. 18%

6. Mark is a dog walker, and he charges a fee of $10 per hour. If he decides to raise his rate by 5%, then what will be his new hourly fee?

   A. $10.50
   B. $11.00
   C. $11.50
   D. $12.00

7. After finishing 20% of his homework, Daniel had 60 questions remaining. How many homework questions were assigned?

   A. 65
   B. 70
   C. 75
   D. 80

8. Megan is invested in a portfolio of stocks, and her investment returns have varied by the following amounts over the past 7 years: 4%, –3%, +5%, –3%, +2%, +6%, –1%. What is the mean of these returns?

   A. 1.43%
   B. 1.57%
   C. 1.69%
   D. 1.74%

9. If fertilizer costs $1.20 per square yard, then how much will it cost to fertilize a 50-foot by 90-foot lawn?

   A. $500
   B. $600
   C. $700
   D. $800

10. Tom wants to build a rectangular log cabin with a perimeter of 200 feet. If the length of the log cabin will be 55 feet, then what will its width be?

   A. 30 feet
   B. 35 feet
   C. 40 feet
   D. 45 feet

11. A half quart of milk represents what portion of a gallon?

   A. One-sixteenth
   B. One-eighth
   C. One-sixth
   D. One-fourth

12. Battery A lasted for 3 years, 12 months, 19 days, 4 hours, and 32 seconds. Battery B lasted for 3 years, 10 months, 11 days, 2 hours, and 13 seconds. How much longer did Battery A last?

    A. 2 months, 8 days, 2 hours, 19 seconds
    B. 2 months, 12 days, 5 hours, 45 seconds
    C. 3 months, 3 days, 4 hours, 19 seconds
    D. 3 months, 8 days, 2 hours, 45 seconds

13. A warehouse worker earns $11 per hour for a 40-hour work week. His overtime pay is two times his base pay. If he worked 44-hours last week, how much did he earn?

    A. $510
    B. $516
    C. $522
    D. $528

14. If a church's bells ring every 30 minutes, then how many times will the bells ring between 11 a.m. and 9 p.m.?

    A. 10
    B. 15
    C. 20
    D. 25

15. A medical clinic orders protective masks by the gross. If the clinic uses 16 masks per day, then how long will the gross last?

    A. 9 days
    B. 12 days
    C. 15 days
    D. 18 days

16. A golfer's recent scores per 18-hole round were 87, 92, 90, 84, and 88. If he wants his average to be 88, then what does he need to score on his next round of golf?

    A. 84
    B. 85
    C. 87
    D. 89

17. Roy is mailing a package that weighs 5.75 pounds. If the shipping cost is $2.20 per pound plus a 5% surcharge, then how much will Roy have to pay to mail his package?

    A. $13.28
    B. $13.97
    C. $14.12
    D. $14.85

18. Todd works as a general contractor and must purchase lumber for three separate jobs. The first job requires 19 feet of lumber, the second job requires 36 inches of lumber, and the third job requires 14 yards of lumber. How many feet of lumber must Todd purchase?

   A. 58
   B. 61
   C. 64
   D. 66

19. Madeline owns a warehouse that she will rent out for $2 per cubic foot per year. If the dimensions of the warehouse are 35 feet (length) by 90 feet (width) by 20 feet (height), then how much will she charge annually for rent?

   A. $101,000
   B. $108,000
   C. $117,000
   D. $126,000

20. Four employees representing 8% of the total staff called in sick for work. How many employees are on the staff?

   A. 40
   B. 50
   C. 60
   D. 70

21. If the minute hand of a clock has moved sixty degrees, then how many minutes have passed?

   A. 5
   B. 10
   C. 15
   D. 20

22. Jody's checking account had a balance of $1,234 at the start of the week. Since then she made a car payment of $231 and a student loan payment of $176. She also deposited her paycheck of $673 and gave $50 to her friend. What is the current balance of Jody's checking account?

   A. $1,215
   B. $1,300
   C. $1,450
   D. $1,525

23. Eight friends dined at a restaurant and the total bill was $175. If they left a 20% tip and split the cost evenly, then how much did each person pay?

A. $26.25
B. $28.10
C. $29.45
D. $31.70

24. Lisa is driving in Canada, where the speed limit is 90 kilometers per hour. If a kilometer equals approximately $\frac{5}{8}$ of a mile, then what is the maximum speed that she can drive without speeding?

A. 53.50 miles per hour
B. 54.75 miles per hour
C. 56.25 miles per hour
D. 58.50 miles per hour

25. At a fast food restaurant, a value meal consists of a cheeseburger ($2.00), an order of fries ($1.50), and a drink ($1.00). What would it cost to feed a family of five, if each person orders a value meal?

A. $22.50
B. $24.50
C. $25.00
D. $26.50

ANSWER KEY

1. C
($36 + $40 + $22 + $33 + $27 + $42) × 0.3 =
$200 × 0.3 = $60

2. D
Distance = rate of speed × time
220 miles = rate of speed × 4 hours
220 miles ÷ 4 hours = rate of speed
55 miles per hour = rate of speed

3. C
Area = ½ base × height
Area = 0.5 × 50 feet × 25 feet = 625 square feet

4. B
Step 1: Find the amount earned from the hourly charge. $230 – $50 = $180
Step 2: Calculate the number of hours worked. $180 ÷ $45 per hour = 4 hours
Four hours after 9 a.m. is 1 p.m.

5. D
Annual interest rate = 1.5% per month × 12 months per year = 18%

6. A
Step 1: Calculate the fee increase. $10.00 × 0.05 = $0.50
Step 2: Find the new hourly fee. $10.00 + $0.50 = $10.50
Alternatively, you could find the answer by $10.00 × 1.05 = $10.50.

7. C
If 20% of the questions have been completed, then 80% of the questions remain. If 80% of the questions is 60, then the original number of questions can be found by cross multiplying.

$$\frac{80\%}{60 \text{ questions}} = \frac{100\%}{x \text{ questions}}$$

80x = 100 × 60
80x = 6,000
x = 75
There were 75 questions assigned.

8. A
Mean = [(4%)+(–3%)+(5%)+(–3%)+(2%)+(6%)+(–1%)] ÷ 7 =
Mean = (4% – 3% + 5% – 3% + 2% + 6% – 1%) ÷ 7 =
Mean = 10% ÷ 7 = 1.43%

9. B
Step 1: Calculate the area in square feet.
50 feet × 90 feet = 4,500 square feet

Step 2: Convert square yards to square feet.
1 square yard = 3 feet × 3 feet = 9 square feet per square yard

Step 3: Calculate the area in square yards.
4,500 square feet ÷ 9 square feet per square yard = 500 square yards

Step 4: Calculate the cost.
500 square yards × $1.20 per square yard = $600

10. D
Perimeter = (2 × length) + (2 × width)
200 feet = (2 × 55 feet) + (2 × width)
200 feet = 110 feet + (2 × width)
90 feet = 2 × width
45 feet = width

11. B
There are four quarts in a gallon, so half a quart is one-eighth of a gallon.

12. A
  3 years, 12 months, 19 days, 4 hours, 32 seconds
$\underline{- \text{3 years, 10 months, 11 days, 2 hours, 13 seconds}}$
             2 months,   8 days, 2 hours, 19 seconds

13. D
Step 1: Calculate the base pay. $11 per hour × 40 hours = $440
Step 2: Calculate the overtime wage. $11 per hour × 2 = $22 per hour
Step 3: Find the number of overtime hours. 44 hours – 40 hours = 4 hours
Step 4: Calculate the overtime pay. $22 per hour × 4 hours = $88
Step 5: Find the total earnings. $440 + $88 = $528

14. C
There are 10 hours between 11 a.m. and 9 p.m. Because the bells ring every 30 minutes, they will ring twice per hour. Therefore, the bells will ring a total of 20 times, found by 10 hours × 2 rings per hour.

15. A
There are 144 masks in a gross, therefore 144 masks ÷ 16 masks per day = 9 days.

16. C
Let x equal the unknown score, then solve for x to find the average.
(87 + 92 + 90 + 84 + 88 + x) ÷ 6 = 88
(441 + x) ÷ 6 = 88
441 + x = 528
x = 87

17. A
Step 1: Calculate the shipping cost. 5.75 pounds × $2.20 per pound = $12.65
Step 2: Calculate the surcharge cost. $12.65 × 0.05 = $0.63
Step 3: Find the total cost. $12.65 + $0.63 = $13.28

18. C
Step 1: Convert inches to feet. 36 inches ÷ 12 inches per foot = 3 feet
Step 2: Convert yards to feet. 14 yards × 3 feet per yard = 42 feet
Step 3: Find the total length. 19 feet + 3 feet + 42 feet = 64 feet

19. D
Step 1: Calculate the volume. 35 feet × 90 feet × 20 feet = 63,000 cubic feet
Step 2: Calculate the annual rent. 63,000 cubic feet × $2 per cubic foot = $126,000

20. B
Let x equal the total number of employees and solve the equation.
$0.08x = 4$
$x = 4 \div 0.08 = 50$
There are 50 employees.

21. B
Because there are 360 degrees in a circle (clock) and 60 minutes in an hour, this problem can be solved by cross multiplying.

$$\frac{60\text{ degrees}}{360\text{ degrees}} = \frac{x\text{ minutes}}{60\text{ minutes}}$$

$60 \times 60 = 360x$
$3,600 = 360x$
$10 = x$
10 minutes have passed.

22. C
$1,234 − $231 − $176 + $673 − $50 = $1,450

23. A
Step 1: Calculate the tip. $175 × 0.2 = $35
Step 2: Find the total cost of the bill. $175 + $35 = $210
Step 3: Calculate each person's payment. $210 ÷ 8 people = $26.25 per person

24. C
90 kilometers per hour $\times \frac{5}{8}$ kilometers per mile = 56.25 miles per hour
Alternatively, divide 5 by 8 to get 0.625, and then multiply by 90 to get 56.25.

25. A
Cost = 5($2.00 + $1.50 + $1.00)
Cost = 5($4.50)
Cost = $22.50

PRACTICE TEST 4

QUESTIONS

1. A bakery begins each morning with 10 dozen bagels available for sale. When their inventory decreases by three-fourths, they begin to bake fresh bagels. How many bagels will be left when it's time to bake a fresh batch?

   A. 30
   B. 35
   C. 40
   D. 45

2. An investment advisor recommended a stock to a client 3 months ago. Since then, the client's original $1,000 investment increased by 20% the first month, 30% the second month, and 10% the third month. What is the current value of the investment?

   A. $1,572
   B. $1,608
   C. $1,716
   D. $1,824

3. Dawn is buying hot dogs for a cookout. If she has $20, and each hot dog pack costs $2.45, then how many packs can she buy?

   A. 7
   B. 8
   C. 9
   D. 10

4. Casey is taking a pop quiz and must answer at least 65% of the questions correctly in order to pass. If the quiz has 20 question, then how many questions can he answer incorrectly and still receive a passing grade?

   A. 5
   B. 6
   C. 7
   D. 8

5. Kelly's work shift begins at 9:30 a.m. She would like to leave her house 40 minutes before her shift begins, and she'd like to wake up 45 minutes before she must leave her house. What time should Kelly wake up?

   A. 8:05 a.m.
   B. 8:10 a.m.
   C. 8:15 a.m.
   D. 8:20 a.m.

6. Between stops, a train traveled 7 miles in 5 minutes. How fast was the train traveling?

   A. 72 miles per hour
   B. 76 miles per hour
   C. 80 miles per hour
   D. 84 miles per hour

7. If Ethan slept for six and a half hours, how many seconds did he sleep?

   A. 22,700
   B. 23,400
   C. 24,200
   D. 25,800

8. A barber earns an average tip of 15% of the cost of each haircut. If her average daily billings to customers total $420, then how much money will she receive in tips?

   A. $63
   B. $76
   C. $464
   D. $483

9. Eric's car gets 20 miles per gallon. If gas costs $2.50 per gallon, then how much will it cost Eric to travel 180 miles?

   A. $21.25
   B. $21.75
   C. $22.00
   D. $22.50

10. An ice cream shop has five large 15-pound bins of ice cream. If each customer receives two-tenths of a pound of ice cream per order, then how many customers can be served if all of the ice cream is used?

   A. 360
   B. 365
   C. 375
   D. 390

11. If there are 3 teaspoons in 1 tablespoon, and 16 tablespoons in 1 cup, then how many teaspoons are in 3 cups?

   A. 48
   B. 96
   C. 144
   D. 192

12. Lindsey and Doug are setting the date for their outdoor wedding, and they're concerned that it might rain. If they're considering four different days in June, and the probability of it raining on any given day is 0.3, then what is the probability that it will not rain on any of the four days?

    A. 0.15
    B. 0.24
    C. 0.27
    D. 0.39

13. A prison guard walks the equivalent of one-half mile when he checks the perimeter of the prison grounds. If he walks at a pace of one mile every 20 minutes, then how long will it take him to complete three laps around the prison grounds?

    A. 30 minutes
    B. 40 minutes
    C. 50 minutes
    D. 60 minutes

14. Of the 60 members of the choir, 35 are girls. Express the ratio of boys to girls as a fraction.

    A. $\frac{2}{7}$
    B. $\frac{3}{7}$
    C. $\frac{4}{7}$
    D. $\frac{5}{7}$

15. An office suite has 15 employees and provides 60 square feet of work space per employee. If 5 additional employees are hired, then how much less work space will each employee have?

    A. 10 square feet
    B. 15 square feet
    C. 20 square feet
    D. 25 square feet

16. Michael's car is about to run out of gas. He checks his pockets and finds two five-dollar bills, three one-dollar bills, three quarters, four dimes, and two nickels. How much gas money does Michael have?

    A. $12.75
    B. $13.25
    C. $14.25
    D. $15.50

17. Ian's bank account balance decreased by 40% last month. By what percent must his bank account increase this month to reach its original starting value?

   A. 33%
   B. 40%
   C. 50%
   D. 67%

18. A loan shark charges $75 of interest the first day a debt is unpaid and $40 for each additional day. If $315 of interest was paid to the loan shark, then how many days was the debt overdue?

   A. 5
   B. 6
   C. 7
   D. 8

19. Francis is holding a bag with 9 yellow balls, 8 purple balls, and 7 orange balls. If Francis randomly selects a ball, what are the odds that it is not purple?

   A. $\dfrac{1}{3}$
   B. $\dfrac{2}{3}$
   C. $\dfrac{3}{4}$
   D. $\dfrac{3}{5}$

20. Lauren would like to build a 5-foot high fence in her backyard. The dimensions of the space that needs to be fenced is 120 feet by 90 feet. If the materials needed to build the fence are $3 per square foot, then how much will Lauren spend on materials?

   A. $4,400
   B. $5,700
   C. $5,900
   D. $6,300

21. A florist sets a price of $40 for a dozen roses. If the florist buys roses from her supplier at a rate of $6 for 4 roses, then how much profit will the florist make if sales total 20 dozen roses for the week?

   A. $440
   B. $560
   C. $680
   D. $800

22. Jason purchased a sailboat and made a down payment of $5,000. If he will pay an additional $300 per month for 6 years, then what is the total cost of the boat?

 A. $6,800
 B. $21,600
 C. $26,600
 D. $29,200

23. Yvonne cuts a circular pizza in half in a straight line. She then eats one slice, creating a 45-degree angle. What is the supplement of that angle?

 A. 45 degrees
 B. 135 degrees
 C. 180 degrees
 D. 225 degrees

24. If 12 cups of sugar are used to bake 10 cakes, then how much sugar is used to bake 2 cakes?

 A. $2\frac{1}{5}$ cups

 B. $2\frac{2}{5}$ cups

 C. $3\frac{3}{5}$ cups

 D. $3\frac{4}{5}$ cups

25. A long-distance runner ran at an average pace of 4 miles per hour for 5 hours. How much time would have been saved if the runner had averaged 5 miles per hour for the same distance?

 A. 1 hour
 B. 2 hours
 C. 3 hours
 D. 4 hours

ANSWER KEY

1. A

Because there are 12 bagels per dozen, there are 120 bagels available for sale at the start of each morning. If the inventory must decrease by three-fourths to begin baking a fresh batch, then one-fourth of the bagels still remain. 120 bagels $\times \frac{1}{4} = 30$ bagels.

2. C

End of month 1: $1,000 \times 0.2 = \$200$. $\$1,000 + \$200 = \$1,200$
End of month 2: $1,200 \times 0.3 = \$360$. $\$1,200 + \$360 = \$1,560$
End of month 3: $1,560 \times 0.1 = \$156$. $\$1,560 + \$156 = \$1,716$

3. B

$\$20 \div \$2.45$ per pack $= 8.16$ packs. Round down to 8 because Dawn can't buy a fraction of a pack.

4. C

Step 1: Calculate the number of questions that must be answered correctly.
$20 \times 0.65 = 13$

Step 2: Find the number of questions that can be answered incorrectly.
$20 - 13 = 7$

5. A

40 minutes before 9:30 a.m. is 8:50 a.m.
45 minutes before 8:50 a.m. is 8:05 a.m.

6. D

Calculate the speed of the car in miles per hour by cross multiplying.

$$\frac{7 \text{ miles}}{5 \text{ minutes}} = \frac{x \text{ miles}}{60 \text{ minutes}}$$

$7 \times 60 = 5x$
$420 = 5x$
$84 = x$
The car is traveling 84 miles per hour.

7. B

6.5 hours $\times$ 60 minutes per hour $\times$ 60 seconds per minute $= 23,400$ seconds

8. A

$\$420 \times 0.15 = \$63$

9. D

Step 1: Calculate the number of gallons needed.
180 miles $\div$ 20 miles per gallon $= 9$ gallons

Step 2: Calculate the cost.
9 gallons $\times \$2.50$ per gallon $= \$22.50$

10. C
Step 1: Calculate the total amount of ice cream.
5 bins × 15 pounds per bin = 75 pounds

Step 2: Calculate the number of customers served.
75 pounds ÷ 0.2 pounds per customer = 375 customers

11. C
3 teaspoons per tablespoon × 16 tablespoons per cup × 3 cups = 144 teaspoons

12. B
If there is a 0.3 probability that it will rain, there is a 0.7 probability that it will not rain. The probability that it will not rain on any of the four days is 0.7 × 0.7 × 0.7 × 0.7 = 0.24

13. A
Step 1: Calculate the number of miles walked. 3 laps × 0.5 miles per lap = 1.5 miles
Step 2: Calculate the number of minutes. 1.5 miles × 20 minutes per mile = 30 minutes

14. D
If there are 60 members of the choir, and 35 are girls, then 25 are boys. The ratio of boys to girls is $\frac{25}{35}$, which can be simplified to $\frac{5}{7}$.

15. B
Step 1: Calculate the area of the work space.
15 employees × 60 square feet per employee = 900 square feet

Step 2: Find the total number of employees.
15 employees + 5 employees = 20 employees

Step 3: Calculate the new work space area per employee.
900 square feet ÷ 20 employees = 45 square feet per employee

Step 4: Find the reduced area for each employee.
60 square feet – 45 square feet = 15 square feet

16. C
2 × $5 = $10
3 × $1 = $3
3 × $0.25 = $0.75
4 × $0.10 = $0.40
2 × $0.05 = $0.10
$10 + $3 + $0.75 + $0.40 + $0.10 = $14.25

17. D
Select a hypothetical starting value for the account, such as $1,000. If the bank account decreased by 40%, then the value decreased by $400 down to $600. The percent change that is required to return the account value back to $1,000 will not be 40%, because 40% of $600 is only $240. Instead the required percent increase will be higher.
Percent change = ($1,000 – $600) ÷ $600
Percent change = $400 ÷ $600 = 66.67% = 67% (rounded)

18. C
Step 1: Find the remaining interest after day 1. $315 – $75 = $240
Step 2: Calculate the number of additional days. $240 ÷ $40 per day = 6 days
Step 3: Find the total number of days. 1 day + 6 days = 7 days

19. B
There are 24 balls in the bag (9 + 8 + 7) and 16 of those are not purple (9 + 7). Therefore, the odds of selecting a ball this is not purple is $\frac{16}{24}$, which can be simplified to $\frac{2}{3}$.

20. D
Step 1: Find the perimeter of the fence. 120 feet + 90 feet + 120 feet + 90 feet = 420 feet
Step 2: Calculate the amount of materials needed. 420 feet × 5 feet = 2,100 square feet
Step 3: Calculate the cost of materials. 2,100 square feet × $3 per square foot = $6,300

21. A
Step 1: Calculate the cost for each rose. $6 ÷ 4 roses = $1.50 per rose
Step 2: Calculate the cost for 20 dozen roses. 20 roses × 12 × $1.50 per rose = $360
Step 3: Calculate the total revenue received. $40 per dozen × 20 dozen = $800
Step 4: Find the profit. $800 – $360 = $440

22. C
Step 1: Calculate the length of the loan. 6 years × 12 months per year = 72 months
Step 2: Calculate the total monthly payments. 72 months × $300 per month = $21,600
Step 3: Find the total cost. $21,600 + $5,000 = $26,600

23. B
Because the pizza is a circle, measuring 360 degrees, half of it measures 180 degrees. The sum of supplementary angles must equal 180 degrees, therefore if one angle is 45 degrees then the other angle must be 135 degrees. 180 degrees – 45 degrees = 135 degrees.

24. B
Calculate the amount of sugar in two cakes by cross multiplying.

$$\frac{12 \text{ cups}}{10 \text{ cakes}} = \frac{x \text{ cups}}{2 \text{ cakes}}$$

$$12 \times 2 = 10x$$

$$24 = 10x$$

$$\frac{24}{10} = \frac{12}{5} = 2\frac{2}{5} = x$$

There are $2\frac{2}{5}$ cups of sugar in two cakes.

25. A
Step 1: Calculate the total distance traveled. 4 miles per hour × 5 hours = 20 miles
Step 2: Calculate the adjusted number of hours. 20 miles ÷ 5 miles per hour = 4 hours
Step 3: Find the amount of time saved. 5 hours – 4 hours = 1 hour

PRACTICE TEST 5

QUESTIONS

1. A car company must make 400 cars per day to keep up with customer demand. If they can make 40 cars per hour, then how many cars still need to be made after 2.5 hours?

   A. 100
   B. 150
   C. 200
   D. 300

2. Rose needs to purchase 3 loaves of bread. She has two coupons, each for 15% off a single loaf. If each loaf has a retail price of $3.00, then how much will Rose spend to purchase 3 loaves?

   A. $8.10
   B. $8.55
   C. $8.85
   D. $9.15

3. If the track surrounding a football field measures one-quarter mile around, then how many laps around the track equals 5.25 miles?

   A. 18
   B. 21
   C. 22
   D. 24

4. Gary's house has a triangular-shaped attic that needs to be heated. If the dimensions of the attic are 30 feet by 10 feet by 55 feet, then what is the volume of space that needs to be heated?

   A. 4,125 cubic feet
   B. 8,250 cubic feet
   C. 12,375 cubic feet
   D. 16,500 cubic feet

5. At a charity fundraiser, Terry runs 5 miles and receives $20 per mile in pledges. If the host of the fundraiser keeps 5% and gives the remaining amount to the charity, then how much money will the charity receive?

   A. $19
   B. $21
   C. $95
   D. $105

6. Logan invests $1,600 in an account that earns 4% annual interest. How much will his account be worth at the end of 8 years?

   A. $1,664
   B. $1,846
   C. $2,060
   D. $2,112

7. Amy earns $1,000 per week for working 40 hours, and double her regular pay when she works overtime. If her weekly pay was $1,300, then how many hours did she work?

   A. 42
   B. 44
   C. 46
   D. 48

8. Jerry needs to purchase 300 chicken wings for a party he is hosting. Which of the following orders will cost Jerry the least amount of money?

   A. Two 150 wing orders at $120 each
   B. Five 60 wing orders at $46 each
   C. Ten 30 wing orders at $27 each
   D. Twenty 15 wing orders at $13 each

9. Over the past 5 days, Richard woke up at 8:10 a.m., 8:45 a.m., 8:25 a.m., 8:55 a.m., and 8:50 a.m. What was the average time that Richard woke up?

   A. 8:37 a.m.
   B. 8:40 a.m.
   C. 8:43 a.m.
   D. 8:47 a.m.

10. A cash register contains $8.50 in nickels and dimes. If there are 115 coins in total, then how many are nickels?

   A. 45
   B. 55
   C. 60
   D. 70

11. Gabe earns an hourly wage of $12.50 per hour, but due to budget cuts his wage will be reduced by 10%. What will be Gabe's new hourly wage?

   A. $11.50
   B. $11.75
   C. $11.00
   D. $11.25

12. Emily has traveled 400 kilometers. If one kilometer equals approximately $\frac{5}{8}$ of a mile, then how many miles has Emily traveled?

    A. 250
    B. 270
    C. 280
    D. 300

13. If "h" inches of snow falls in one hour, then how many inches fall in "d" days?

    A. 24hd
    B. 24h ÷ d
    C. 24h × 365d
    D. 365 ÷ 24h

14. Nick was told that the value of his new car will depreciate at a rate of 10% per year. If he paid $30,000 for the car last week, then what will its value be after three years?

    A. $19,683
    B. $21,870
    C. $24,300
    D. $27,000

15. A plumber needs 16 lengths of pipe, each measuring 9.5 feet long. If pipe is sold for $2.50 per foot, then how much will the total quantity of pipe cost?

    A. $350
    B. $370
    C. $380
    D. $400

16. If Tom rides his scooter at a constant speed of 16 miles per hour, then how many miles will he have traveled in 24 minutes?

    A. 5.9
    B. 6.4
    C. 6.8
    D. 7.3

17. A 12-inch by 16-inch canvas has been painted, and a 1-inch frame has been added. What is the area of the painting that is visible inside the frame?

    A. 110 square inches
    B. 120 square inches
    C. 130 square inches
    D. 140 square inches

18. Train A leaves the station at 9:00 a.m., moving east at 60 miles per hour. At 9:30 a.m., Train B leaves the station moving the same direction on a parallel track. How fast must Train B travel in order to catch up with Train A at 1:30 p.m.?

    A. 62.5 miles per hour
    B. 65.5 miles per hour
    C. 67.5 miles per hour
    D. 70.5 miles per hour

19. A publishing company brought 1,250 books to a book fair. 350 people attended, and after the book fair ended there were 200 books remaining. What was the average number of books that each person bought?

    A. 3
    B. 4
    C. 5
    D. 6

20. Mark, Luke, and Tom work the same shift together in a factory. If Luke made twice as many products as Mark, and Tom made three more products than Mark, then how many products did Mark make if 39 products were made between the three of them?

    A. 8
    B. 9
    C. 10
    D. 11

21. Jessica is driving from Louisville, KY to Little Rock, AR for a job interview. If the distance between the two cities is 510 miles, and Jessica drives at an average speed of 60 miles per hour, then how long will it take her to drive to Little Rock?

    A. 8 hours 30 minutes
    B. 8 hours 45 minutes
    C. 9 hours 15 minutes
    D. 9 hours 30 minutes

22. A stockbroker receives a bi-weekly salary of $1,500, plus an 8% commission on all stock sales made during the period. If the broker sold stock totaling $15,000, then what is the ratio of the broker's commission to her salary?

    A. 2:3
    B. 3:4
    C. 4:5
    D. 5:6

23. Jackie left home for a short trip at 7 a.m. and returned 56 hours later. What time did she arrive back home?

   A. 9 a.m.
   B. 12 a.m.
   C. 3 p.m.
   D. 5 p.m.

24. Dominic is fencing a rectangular garden that is half as wide as it is long. If the total perimeter is 180 feet, then what is its width?

   A. 15 feet
   B. 30 feet
   C. 45 feet
   D. 60 feet

25. A pharmacist earns an annual salary of $95,000. If she pays federal income tax equal to 24% of her gross pay, then what is her net pay?

   A. $22,800
   B. $57,400
   C. $65,600
   D. $72,200

ANSWER KEY

1. D
Step 1: Calculate the number of cars made in 2.5 hours by cross multiplying.

$$\frac{40 \text{ cars}}{1 \text{ hour}} = \frac{x \text{ cars}}{2.5 \text{ hours}}$$

$40 \times 2.5 = 1x$
$100 = x$

Step 2: Find the number of cars that still need to be made. 400 cars – 100 cars = 300 cars

2. A
Step 1: Calculate the price for each discounted loaf of bread.
$\$3.00 \times 0.15 = \$0.45$
$\$3.00 – \$0.45 = \$2.55$

Step 2: Find the total cost for 3 loaves.
$\$2.55 + \$2.55 + \$3.00 = \$8.10$

3. B
If the track is one-quarter mile around, then 4 laps equals 1 mile.
5.25 miles × 4 laps per mile = 21 laps

4. B
Volume of a triangle = ½ base × height × length
Volume of a triangle = 0.5 × 30 feet × 10 feet × 55 feet = 8,250 cubic feet

5. C
Step 1: Calculate the amount raised by Terry. 5 miles × $20 per mile = $100
Step 2: Calculate the amount paid to the charity. $100 × 0.95 = $95

6. D
Step 1: Calculate the interest for 8 years by using the formula I = Prt, where I = interest, P = principal, r = rate of interest, and t = time.
I = Prt
I = ($1,600)(0.04)(8) = $512

Step 2: Find the total account value. $1,600 + $512 = $2,112

7. C
Step 1: Calculate Amy's regular hourly wage.
$1,000 per week ÷ 40 hours per week = $25 per hour

Step 2: Calculate Amy's overtime hourly wage.
$25 per hour × 2 = $50 per hour

Step 3: Calculate the number of overtime hours worked.
($1,300 – $1,000) ÷ $50 per hour =
$300 ÷ $50 per hour = 6 hours

Step 4: Find the total number of hours that Amy worked.
40 hours + 6 hours = 46 hours

8. B
Option A: 2 × $120 = $240
Option B: 5 × $46 = $230
Option C: 10 × $27 = $270
Option D: 20 × $13 = $260
Option B is the cheapest, which is five 60 wing orders for $46 each.

9. A
Since each time was between 8 a.m. and 9 a.m., add up the minutes and divide by 5 to find the average.
Average time = (10 minutes + 45 minutes + 25 minutes + 55 minutes + 50 minutes) ÷ 5
Average time = 185 minutes ÷ 5 = 37 minutes
The average time that Richard woke up was 8:37 a.m.

10. C
Let n equal the number of nickels, and 115 – n equal the number of dimes. The equation can be expressed as: [nickel value × n] + [dime value × (115 – n)] = $8.50
$0.05n + [$0.1(115 – n)] = $8.50
$0.05n + $11.50 – $0.1n = $8.50
$–0.05n = –$3
n = 60
The cash register contains 60 nickels.

11. D
Step 1: Calculate the wage reduction. $12.50 × 0.1 = $1.25
Step 2: Find Gabe's new hourly wage. $12.50 – $1.25 = $11.25

12. A
400 kilometers × $\frac{5}{8}$ kilometers per mile = 250 miles
Alternatively, you could multiply 400 by 5 and then divide the answer by 8 to get 250.

13. A
To find the amount of snow that falls in one day, multiply the amount that falls in one hour by 24, because there are 24 hours in a day. Therefore, in d days, the amount of snow that falls can be expressed as 24 × h × d or 24hd.

14. B
If the car depreciates 10% the first year, then the value of the car will be 90% of its original value. The process repeats each year.
Value after year 1: $30,000 × 0.9 = $27,000
Value after year 2: $27,000 × 0.9 = $24,300
Value after year 3: $24,300 × 0.9 = $21,870

15. C
Step 1: Calculate the amount of pipe needed. 16 × 9.5 feet = 152 feet
Step 2: Calculate the price. 152 feet × $2.50 per foot = $380

16. B
Step 1: Convert minutes to hours.
24 minutes ÷ 60 minutes per hour = 0.4 hours

Step 2: Calculate the distance traveled.
Distance = rate of speed × time
Distance = 16 miles per hour × 0.4 hours = 6.4 miles

17. D
The canvas is 12 inches by 16 inches, and after subtracting the 1-inch frame from all four sides, the dimensions inside the frame are 10 inches by 14 inches. (Remember that by subtracting 1 inch from each side you are subtracting 2 inches from the length and 2 inches from the width.) The area of the painting that is visible inside the frame can be found by multiplying 10 inches by 14 inches. 10 inches × 14 inches = 140 square inches

18. C
Step 1: By the time Train B leaves the station, Train A has already been traveling for 30 minutes, or 0.5 hours. Train A therefore traveled 4.5 hours at a rate of 60 miles per hour, for a total distance of 270 miles. (4.5 hours × 60 miles per hour = 270 miles)

Step 2: Train B has 4 hours to travel 270 miles to catch up with Train A. Therefore it must travel 67.5 miles per hour. (270 miles ÷ 4 hours = 67.5 miles per hour)

19. A
Step 1: Find the number of books sold.
1,250 books – 200 books = 1,050 books

Step 2: Calculate the average number of books that each person bought.
1,050 books ÷ 350 people = 3 books per person

20. B
Let Mark's production equal y. Therefore Luke's production is 2y and Tom's production is y + 3.

y + 2y + y + 3 = 39
4y + 3 = 39
4y = 36
y = 9
Mark made 9 products during his shift.

21. A
510 miles ÷ 60 miles per hour = 8.5 hours, which is equal to 8 hours 30 minutes.

22. C
Step 1: Calculate the commission: $15,000 × 0.08 = $1,200
Step 2: Find the ratio of commission to salary: $\frac{\$1,200}{\$1,500} = \frac{4}{5} = 4:5$

23. C
If Jackie left home at 7 a.m., then 48 hours later it would be 7 a.m. again. That leaves eight additional hours. Eight hours after 7 a.m. is 3 p.m.

24. B
Let L = length and W = width.
Perimeter = 2L + 2W
180 feet = 2L + 2(0.5L)
180 feet = 2L + 1L
180 feet = 3L
60 feet = L
Because the length is 60 feet, the width is one-half, or 30 feet.

25. D
Step 1: Calculate the taxes paid. $95,000 × 0.24 = $22,800
Step 2: Find the net pay. $95,000 – $22,800 = $72,200
Alternatively, you could multiply $95,000 by 0.76 to get $72,200.

PRACTICE TEST 6

QUESTIONS

1. If the population of a city grew by 10,000 people last year, which was 25% more than the city planner had predicted, then the population was originally estimated to grow by how many people?

   A. 6,500
   B. 7,000
   C. 7,500
   D. 8,000

2. Joan is holding a balloon on a string that has blown to a position directly over Jason's head. If Jason is standing 6 feet away from Joan, and the balloon is flying 8 feet in the air, then what is the length of the balloon string?

   A. 8 feet
   B. 9 feet
   C. 10 feet
   D. 12 feet

3. At Bagels-R-Us, one bagel normally costs $2, but this week they are offering a special price of five bagels for $8. If Monica purchases 20 bagels, how much more would she have paid if she didn't take advantage of the offer?

   A. $8
   B. $9
   C. $10
   D. $11

4. A bartender earns an average tip of 20% of each customer's drink order. However, he must give 25% of his tips to the bar owner. If the total customer orders for the night are $1,400, then how much in tips will the bartender get to keep?

   A. $180
   B. $200
   C. $210
   D. $230

5. A food truck sells sandwiches for $5 each. If one sandwich costs $3 to make, and the food truck owner must pay his employee $80 per day to operate the truck, then how many sandwiches must be sold each day to make a profit?

   A. 38
   B. 39
   C. 40
   D. 41

6. If an 8-person construction crew can build 4 condos per year, then how many condos can a 20-person crew be expected to build?

    A. 8
    B. 9
    C. 10
    D. 11

7. A company is installing hardwood floors in each of its four conference rooms. If the dimensions of the four rooms (in feet) are 12 × 15, 11 × 14, 12 × 14, and 13 × 15, then what is the total amount of hardwood flooring that will be installed?

    A. 684 square feet
    B. 697 square feet
    C. 713 square feet
    D. 728 square feet

8. If the moon is 238,900 miles from Earth, and it takes 1.284 seconds for moonlight to reach Earth, then approximately how fast does light travel?

    A. 167,000 miles per second
    B. 175,000 miles per second
    C. 186,000 miles per second
    D. 198,000 miles per second

9. Frank deposited $150 in an account that earns 10% interest per year. Assuming no money has been withdrawn, how much interest will be earned in the second year?

    A. $16.50
    B. $18.25
    C. $19.75
    D. $20.25

10. Jerry's lunch bill is $14.00. If sales tax is 6% and he leaves a 15% tip on the pre-tax bill, then how much will Jerry pay in total?

    A. $15.12
    B. $15.86
    C. $16.94
    D. $17.83

11. If a car salesman sold 55 cars this year and 45 last year, then what percent fewer cars did he sell last year?

    A. 17%
    B. 22%
    C. 25%
    D. 29%

12. Jefferson High School is required by the county to serve meals to students that weigh 20 ounces each. If the school receives a food delivery that includes one ton of food, how many meals can be served?

    A. 1,000
    B. 1,200
    C. 1,400
    D. 1,600

13. Two basketball teams will each play 16 games this season. Team A has won 6 of their first 8 games., and Team B has won 4 of their first 8 games. If Team B wins 75% of their remaining games, then how many of the remaining games must Team A win to finish the season with one more victory than Team B?

    A. 4
    B. 5
    C. 6
    D. 7

14. By switching cable providers, the Jones family can save an average of 7% each month on their cable bill. If their average bill used to be $118.40 per month, then what will be the amount of their new bill?

    A. $109.38
    B. $110.11
    C. $113.45
    D. $114.92

15. A chemist is mixing a formula that requires 225 milliliters of liquid. If the liquid is currently in a two-liter bottle, then what percent of the bottle should be poured into the formula?

    A. 11.25%
    B. 12.75%
    C. 13.50%
    D. 14.00%

16. If Renee rolls 3 six-sided dice, what is the probability of her not rolling a 2?

    A. $\dfrac{105}{196}$

    B. $\dfrac{115}{208}$

    C. $\dfrac{125}{216}$

    D. $\dfrac{135}{264}$

17. A shipping crate that contains 5 computer printers weighs 81 pounds 12 ounces in total. If each printer weights 12 pounds 2 ounces, then how much does the shipping crate weigh?

    A. 19 pounds 6 ounces
    B. 20 pounds 8 ounces
    C. 21 pounds 2 ounces
    D. 22 pounds 4 ounces

18. A patient's medication must be administered every three hours for a total of five times. If the first dose is given at 7 a.m., then what time will the final dose be administered?

    A. 4 p.m.
    B. 5 p.m.
    C. 6 p.m.
    D. 7 p.m.

19. Andy, Jake, and Josh operate a math tutoring business. Andy charges $20 per hour, Jake charges $18 per hour, and Josh charges $16 per hour. If they worked the same number of hours and their combined revenue for the day was $378, then how long did each person work?

    A. 5 hours
    B. 7 hours
    C. 8 hours
    D. 9 hours

20. The price of a ticket to a single baseball game is $22, and the price of a season pass for 80 games is $1,440. Assuming that all 80 games will be attended, how much money will the ticket holder save if she purchases the season pass?

    A. $320
    B. $340
    C. $350
    D. $370

21. Jeff is taking a midterm exam and needs to answer at least 48 of the 80 questions correctly to receive a passing grade. What percent of the questions can Jeff answer incorrectly and still pass the exam?

    A. 30%
    B. 35%
    C. 40%
    D. 45%

22. A factory imports 23,600 pounds of raw material and must pay a tariff equal to $0.20 per pound. What is the amount of the tariff the factory must pay?

    A. $4,720
    B. $4,845
    C. $5,260
    D. $5,615

23. An electric car travels 200 miles at a rate of 50 miles per hour, and then 75 miles at a rate of 75 miles per hour. What was the car's average speed for the trip?

    A. 55 miles per hour
    B. 50 miles per hour
    C. 55 miles per hour
    D. 60 miles per hour

24. A rare coin dealer bought a coin for $130 and sold it the next day for $45 more than the purchase price. What was the percent profit on the sale?

    A. 35%
    B. 40%
    C. 45%
    D. 50%

25. Taylor would like to carpet a room that measures 12 feet by 15 feet. If the price of carpet is $30 per square yard, then what is the total cost to carpet the room?

    A. $580
    B. $600
    C. $610
    D. $630

ANSWER KEY

1. D

The population grew by 25% more than the amount estimated. Therefore, the actual population growth can be expressed as $1 + 25\%$, or 1.25. Next, solve for the expected population growth by using the equation $1.25x = 10,000$. Solve for x by dividing both sides of the equation by 1.25. Therefore $x = 8,000$.

2. C

Solve by using the Pythagorean theorem: $a^2 + b^2 = c^2$

$(6 \text{ feet})^2 + (8 \text{ feet})^2 = c^2$

36 square feet $+$ 64 square feet $= c^2$

100 square feet $= c^2$

10 feet $= c$

3. A

Step 1: Calculate the price per bagel at the discounted price.
$8 \div 5$ bagels $= \$1.60$ per bagel

Step 2: Calculate the price for 20 bagels at the discounted price.
$1.60 per bagel $\times$ 20 bagels $= \$32$

Step 3: Calculate the price for 20 bagels without the discount.
$2 per bagel $\times$ 20 bagels $= \$40$

Step 4: Find the difference in price.
$40 – \$32 = \$8

4. C

Step 1: Calculate the total amount of tips. $1,400 \times 0.2 = \$280$
Step 2: Calculate the amount of tips that must be paid to the owner. $280 \times 0.25 = \$70$
Step 3: Find the amount the bartender keeps. $280 – \$70 = \$210$

5. D

Step 1: Find the profit per sandwich.
$5 – \$3 = \$2

Step 2: Calculate the number of sandwiches that must be sold to break even.
$80 \div \$2$ per sandwich $= 40$ sandwiches (If 40 sandwiches must be sold to break even, then at least 41 sandwiches must be sold to make a profit.)

6. C

If an 8-person crew can build 4 condos per year, cross multiply to determine how many condos a 20-person crew can be expected to build.

$$\frac{8 \text{ people}}{4 \text{ condos}} = \frac{20 \text{ people}}{x \text{ condos}}$$

$8x = 4 \times 20$

$8x = 80$

$x = 10$

A 20-person crew can be expected to build 10 condos per year.

7. B
Room 1: 12 feet × 15 feet = 180 square feet
Room 2: 11 feet × 14 feet = 154 square feet
Room 3: 12 feet × 14 feet = 168 square feet
Room 4: 13 feet × 15 feet = 195 square feet
180 + 154 + 168 + 195 = 697 square feet

8. C
Distance = rate of speed × time
238,900 miles = rate of speed × 1.284 seconds
186,000 miles per second = rate of speed

9. A
Year 1 value = $150.00 × 1.1 = $165.00
Year 2 value = $165.00 × 1.1 = $181.50
Interest earned in second year = $181.50 – $165.00 = $16.50

10. C
Step 1: Calculate the sales tax. $14.00 × 0.06 = $0.84
Step 2: Calculate the tip. $14.00 × 0.15 = $2.10
Step 3: Find the total. $14.00 + $0.84 + $2.10 = $16.94

11. B
Percent change = (new amount – old amount) ÷ old amount
Percent change = (55 cars – 45 cars) ÷ 45 cars
Percent change = 10 cars ÷ 45 cars = 0.22 = 22%

12. D
Because there are 16 ounces in a pound and 2,000 pounds in a ton, the delivery contains 32,000 ounces of food (2,000 pounds × 16 ounces per pound = 32,000 ounces). Each meal must be 20 ounces, therefore the delivery can serve 1,600 meals (32,000 ounces ÷ 20 ounces per meal = 1,600 meals).

13. B
If Team B wins 75% of their remaining 8 games, that equals 6 victories. That would bring Team B's total victories to 10. Team A must therefore win 11 games to finish the season with one more victory than Team B. Since Team A already has 6 victories, they need to win 5 more games.

14. B
Step 1: Calculate the savings. $118.40 × 0.07 = $8.29
Step 2: Find the new monthly bill: $118.40 – $8.29 = $110.11
Alternatively, $118.40 × 0.93 = $110.11

15. A
One liter contains 1,000 milliliters, therefore two liters contains 2,000 milliliters.
225 milliliters ÷ 2,000 milliliters = 0.1125 = 11.25%

16. C
Because the probability of rolling a 2 is $\frac{1}{6}$, the probability of not rolling a 2 is $\frac{5}{6}$.
$$\frac{5}{6} \times \frac{5}{6} \times \frac{5}{6} = \frac{125}{216}$$

17. C
Step 1: Calculate the weight of the printers.
12 pounds 2 ounces × 5 = 60 pounds 10 ounces

Step 2: Find the weight of the shipping crate.
   81 pounds 12 ounces
− 60 pounds 10 ounces
   21 pounds   2 ounces

18. D
The doses would be administered at 7 a.m., 10 a.m., 1 p.m., 4 p.m., and 7 p.m. Therefore, the final dose would be administered at 7 p.m.

19. B
Step 1: Find the combined hourly wage. $20 + $18 + $16 = $54
Step 2: Calculate the number of hours. $378 ÷ $54 per hour = 7 hours

20. A
Step 1: Calculate the price without the season pass: 80 games × $22 per game = $1,760
Step 2: Find the money saved with the season pass: $1,760 − $1,440 = $320

21. C
Step 1: Find the number of questions that can be answered incorrectly.
80 questions − 48 questions = 32 questions

Step 2: Calculate the percentage.
32 questions ÷ 80 questions = 40%

22. A
23,600 × $0.20 = $4,720

23. C
Step 1: Calculate the total amount of time the car traveled.
200 miles ÷ 50 miles per hour = 4 hours
75 miles ÷ 75 miles per hour = 1 hours
4 hours + 1 hour = 5 hours

Step 2: Find the total distance traveled.
200 miles + 75 miles = 275 miles

Step 3: Calculate the average speed.
275 miles ÷ 5 hours = 55 miles per hour

24. A
$45 ÷ $130 = 35%

25. B
Step 1: Calculate the area in square feet.
12 feet × 15 feet = 180 square feet

Step 2: Convert square yards to square feet.
1 square yard = 3 feet × 3 feet = 9 square feet

Step 3: Calculate the area in square yards.
180 square feet ÷ 9 square feet per square yard = 20 square yards

Step 4: Calculate the cost.
20 square yards × $30 per square yard = $600

PART 2

MATHEMATICS KNOWLEDGE

PRACTICE TEST 1

QUESTIONS

1. If x = 6, what is the value of z in the equation z = (x² ÷ 2) – 5?

   A. 1
   B. 4
   C. 13
   D. 16

2. 70% of 40 is 25% of what number?

   A. 7
   B. 28
   C. 56
   D. 112

3. $\sqrt{144} \div \sqrt{36} \times \sqrt{25} + \sqrt{16} - \sqrt{9} =$

   A. 11
   B. 13
   C. 16
   D. 20

4. If the average of 17, 21, 30, 44, 51, and x is 31, what is the value of x?

   A. 21
   B. 23
   C. 26
   D. 27

5. If a circle has a radius of 72, what is its circumference rounded to the nearest whole number?

   A. 46
   B. 113
   C. 226
   D. 452

6. A cube has a volume of 8 cubic inches. What is its surface area?

   A. 24 square inches
   B. 32 square inches
   C. 64 square inches
   D. 72 square inches

7. $2.1 \times 10^4 =$

    A. 2,100
    B. 21,000
    C. 210,000
    D. 2,100,000

8. $(x + 5)(x + 3) =$

    A. $x + 8x + 15$
    B. $x + 15x + 8$
    C. $x^2 + 8x + 15$
    D. $x^2 + 15x + 8$

9. What is the area of figure XYZ?

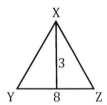

    A. 11
    B. 12
    C. 16
    D. 24

10. Simplify $\sqrt{64x^2}$

    A. $8x$
    B. $16x$
    C. $32x$
    D. $64x$

11. Which of the following can be rewritten as the product of 16 and c is equal to 12 more than b?

    A. $16 \div c = 12 - b$
    B. $16 \div c = b + 12$
    C. $16c = 12 - b$
    D. $16c = b + 12$

12. Solve for x: $5(4x - 6) - 3(1x + 5) = -3(x + 7) - 4$

    A. –1
    B. 0
    C. 1
    D. 2

13. $5\frac{1}{2} + 4\frac{1}{6} + 7\frac{3}{12} =$

    A. $16\frac{5}{6}$
    B. $16\frac{11}{12}$
    C. $17\frac{3}{8}$
    D. $17\frac{5}{9}$

14. The number 0.24 is what percent of 0.8?

    A. 26%
    B. 30%
    C. 34%
    D 42%

15. If $4y^2 = 36$, then y can equal which of the following?

    A. +3 or –3
    B. +4 or –4
    C. +5 or –3
    D. +6 or –2

16. A circle has a circumference of 6.28. What is its diameter?

    A. 1
    B. 1.5
    C. 2
    D. 3.5

17. Solve for x: $(4 \times 2)(72 \div 36)(3 + 5)(61 - 57) = x^3$

    A. 8
    B. 12
    C. 16
    D. 20

18. If lines A and B are parallel, then the following figure is what type of quadrilateral?

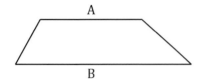

A. Equilateral
B. Parallelogram
C. Rhombus
D. Trapezoid

19. If $x - 3y = 5x + y$, and both sides of the equation equal 12, what is the value of x?

A. 2
B. 3
C. 4
D. 5

20. $\sqrt{441}$ is a number between:

A. 18 and 20
B. 20 and 22
C. 22 and 24
D. 24 and 26

21. In the number 351.924, which digit is in the tenths place?

A. 1
B. 2
C. 4
D. 9

22. Which of the following is the quotient of 6.75 and 0.045?

A. 135
B. 150
C. 160
D. 175

23. What is the prime factorization of 72?

A. $2^3 \times 3^2$
B. $2^4 \times 3^3$
C. $4^2 \times 3^2$
D. $4^3 \times 3^2$

24. If $p = \dfrac{1}{2}$, what is the value of y when $\dfrac{y}{12} = \dfrac{4}{p}$?

    A. 42
    B. 64
    C. 96
    D. 128

25. Solve for x: $5x - 4 = 2x + 8$

    A. 1
    B. 3
    C. 4
    D. 6

ANSWER KEY

1. C

Substitute 6 for x in the equation and then solve for z.

$z = (x^2 \div 2) - 5$

$z = (6^2 \div 2) - 5$

$z = (36 \div 2) - 5$

$z = 18 - 5 = 13$

2. D

Rewrite as an equation and solve.

$0.7 \times 40 = 0.25 \times y$

$28 = 0.25y$

$28 \div 0.25 = y$

$112 = y$

3. A

$\sqrt{144} \div \sqrt{36} \times \sqrt{25} + \sqrt{16} - \sqrt{9} =$

$12 \div 6 \times 5 + 4 - 3 =$

$2 \times 5 + 4 - 3 =$

$10 + 4 - 3 = 11$

4. B

Write the equation as if you're finding the average and then substitute x for the missing number and solve.

$(17 + 21 + 30 + 44 + 51 + x) \div 6 = 31$

$(163 + x) \div 6 = 31$

$163 + x = 186$

$x = 23$

5. D

Circumference $= 2 \times \pi \times$ radius

Circumference $= 2 \times 3.14 \times 72 = 452.16 = 452$ (rounded)

6. A

Step 1: One edge of the cube must be 2 inches long, because 2 is the cube root of 8.
2 inches $\times$ 2 inches $\times$ 2 inches = 8 cubic inches

Step 2: If one of the edges is 2 inches, then the area of each face must be 4 square inches.
2 inches $\times$ 2 inches = 4 square inches

Step 3: Because there are six sides to a cube, the total surface area is 24 square inches.
4 square inches $\times$ 6 = 24 square inches

7. B

$2.1 \times 10^4 =$

$2.1 \times (10 \times 10 \times 10 \times 10) =$

$2.1 \times 10,000 = 21,000$

8. C
Solve by using the FOIL (First, Outer, Inner, Last) method.
Step 1: Multiply the first variable in the first set of parentheses by the first variable in the second set of parentheses: $(x)(x) = x^2$

Step 2: Multiply the first variable in the first set of parentheses by the second number in the second set of parentheses: $(x)(3) = 3x$

Step 3: Multiply the second number in the first set of parentheses by the first variable in the second set of parenthesis: $(5)(x) = 5x$

Step 4: Multiply the second number in the first set of parentheses by the second number in the second set of parentheses: $(5)(3) = 15$

Step 5: Add the steps together to get $x^2 + 3x + 5x + 15 = x^2 + 8x + 15$

9. B
Area = ½ base × height
Area = $0.5 \times 8 \times 3 = 12$

10. A
$64x^2$ can be rewritten as $(8x)^2$. Then pull out the terms from under the radical, so $\sqrt{(8x)^2}$ becomes 8x.

11. D
The product of 16 and c is equal to 12 more than b can be rewritten as $16c = b + 12$

12. C
$5(4x - 6) - 3(1x + 5) = -3(x + 7) - 4$
$20x - 30 - 3x - 15 = -3x - 21 - 4$
$17x - 45 = -3x - 25$
$20x = 20$
$x = 1$

13. B
Convert to the lowest common denominator, which is 12, and then add the fractions.
$5\frac{1}{2} + 4\frac{1}{6} + 7\frac{3}{12} =$
$5\frac{6}{12} + 4\frac{2}{12} + 7\frac{3}{12} = 16\frac{11}{12}$

14. B
$0.24 \div 0.8 = 0.3 = 30\%$

15. A
$4y^2 = 36$
$y^2 = 36 \div 4$
$y^2 = 9$
$y = +3$ or -3

16. C
Circumference = π × diameter
6.28 = 3.14 × diameter
2 = diameter

17. A
$(4 \times 2)(72 \div 36)(3 + 5)(61 - 57) = x^3$
$(8)(2)(8)(4) = x^3$
$512 = x^3$
$8 = x$

18. D
A trapezoid is a quadrilateral with only one pair of parallel sides.

19. B
Step 1: Solve the left side of the equation.
$x - 3y = 12$
$x = 12 + 3y$

Step 2: Substitute the value for x from step 1 into the right side of the equation.
$5x + y = 12$
$5(12 + 3y) + y = 12$
$60 + 15y + y = 12$
$60 + 16y = 12$
$16y = -48$
$y = -3$

Step 3: Substitute the value of y to find the value of x.
$x - 3y = 12$
$x - (3)(-3) = 12$
$x + 9 = 12$
$x = 3$

20. B
This problem can be answered through backsolving. If $20^2 = 400$, and $22^2 = 484$, then $\sqrt{441}$ lies between 20 and 22.

21. D
3 is in the hundreds place
5 is in the tens place
1 is in the ones place
9 is in the tenths place
2 is in the hundredths place
4 is in the thousands place

22. B
Move the decimal point three places to the right in the numerator and denominator to create whole numbers and then divide.

$$\frac{6.75}{0.045} = \frac{6,750}{45} = 150$$

23. A
$72 =$
$36 \times 2 =$
$18 \times 2 \times 2 =$
$9 \times 2 \times 2 \times 2 =$
$3 \times 3 \times 2 \times 2 \times 2 =$
$2^3 \times 3^2$

24. C
Step 1: Convert $\frac{1}{2}$ to a decimal and substitute for p.
$$\frac{y}{12} = \frac{4}{0.5}$$
Step 2: Cross multiply and solve for y.
$0.5y = 4 \times 12$
$0.5y = 48$
$y = 96$

25. C
$5x - 4 = 2x + 8$
$3x - 4 = 8$
$3x = 12$
$x = 4$

PRACTICE TEST 2

QUESTIONS

1. If a rectangle has a perimeter of 28 and a width of 6, what is its area?

    A. 34
    B. 40
    C. 48
    D. 56

2. If $p + q = 8$, what is the value of $6p + 6q + 9$?

    A. 39
    B. 45
    C. 51
    D. 57

3. Solve for x: $-20x + 4 = 5(x - 3) - 8(4x - 5)$

    A. 3
    B. 4
    C. 6
    D. 7

4. If $I = Prt$, and $P = \$10,000$, $r = 4.5\%$, and $t = 1$, what does I equal?

    A. $45
    B. $450
    C. $4,500
    D. $45,000

5. $0.572 \times 10^3 =$

    A. 5.72
    B. 57.2
    C. 572
    D. 5,720

6. $\sqrt{81} \times \sqrt{36} =$

    A. 45
    B. 54
    C. 63
    D. 72

7. What is 40 percent of 95?

   A. 38
   B. 42
   C. 43
   D. 46

8. If $70 \div y = 5z$, what is the value of zy?

   A. 10
   B. 11
   C. 14
   D. 17

9. If the measure of an angle is 36 degrees, what is the complement of the angle?

   A. 36 degrees
   B. 54 degrees
   C. 144 degrees
   D. 324 degrees

10. The following angle appears to be which of the following?

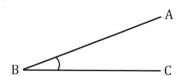

   A. Acute
   B. Obtuse
   C. Right
   D. Straight

11. 25% of 30% of 400 is:

   A. 27
   B. 30
   C. 34
   D. 39

12. The product of two consecutive even numbers is 288. What are the numbers?

   A. 12, 14
   B. 14, 16
   C. 15, 17
   D. 16, 18

13. Which of the following fractions is closest in value to 0.70?

    A. $\dfrac{2}{3}$

    B. $\dfrac{4}{7}$

    C. $\dfrac{5}{8}$

    D. $\dfrac{7}{9}$

14. Solve for y: $9(7y + 4) + 7(5y - 1) = -8(y + 4) + 8$

    A. -1

    B. $-\dfrac{1}{2}$

    C. $\dfrac{1}{2}$

    D. 2

15. How many factors does the number 96 have?

    A. 12
    B. 14
    C. 15
    D. 18

16. Simplify $\dfrac{18x^9}{6x^6}$

    A. $3x^3$
    B. $3x^{1.5}$
    C. $6x^2$
    D. $18x^3$

17. Which of the following fractions is the smallest?

    A. $\dfrac{2}{5}$

    B. $\dfrac{3}{10}$

    C. $\dfrac{5}{15}$

    D. $\dfrac{4}{20}$

18. If n = q, then 7 – 2(n – q) =

    A. 2
    B. 5
    C. 7
    D. 9

19. (12 – 6y) – (9y – 15) =

    A. 3 + 3y
    B. 3 – 3y
    C. 27 + 15y
    D. 27 – 15y

20. If y = 4, then $y^4 \div 4y + y =$

    A. 5
    B. 20
    C. 22
    D. 40

21. The fifth root of 1,024 is:

    A. 2
    B. 3
    C. 4
    D. 6

22. If ABCD is a square, what is the value of x?

    A. 5
    B. 6
    C. 8
    D. 10

23. $1.5 \times 6^3 =$

    A. 54
    B. 324
    C. 648
    D. 729

24. Solve for x: $(7 + 3)(6 \div 2)(9 - 4) = (4 + 1)x$

    A. 18
    B. 24
    C. 26
    D. 30

25. $3(\sqrt{196} \div \sqrt{49}) =$

    A. 6
    B. 9
    C. 12
    D. 15

ANSWER KEY

1. C
Step 1: Perimeter = (2 × length) + (2 × width)
28 = (2 × length) + (2 × 6)
28 = (2 × length) + 12
28 – 12 = 2 × length
16 = 2 × length
8 = length

Step 2: Area = length × width
Area = 8 × 6 = 48

2. D
If p + q = 8, then p = 8 – q. Substitute 8 – q for p and solve.
6p + 6q + 9 =
6(8 – q) + 6q + 9 =
48 – 6q + 6q + 9 =
48 + 9 = 57

3. A
–20x + 4 = 5x – 15 – 32x + 40
–20x + 4 = –27x + 25
7x = 21
x = 3

4. B
I = Prt
I = ($10,000)(4.5%)(1)
I = ($10,000)(0.045)(1) = $450

5. C
$0.572 \times 10^3 =$
0.572 × 10 × 10 × 10 =
0.572 × 1,000 = 572
Alternatively, you could move the decimal point three places to the right because 10 is raised to the third power. Therefore 0.572 becomes 572.

6. B
$\sqrt{81} \times \sqrt{36} =$
9 × 4 = 54

7. A
0.4 × 95 = 38

8. C
70 ÷ y = 5z
70 = 5zy
14 = zy

9. B
To find the complement of an angle, subtract the angle's measurement from 90 degrees.
90 degrees – 36 degrees = 54 degrees

10. A
The angle is acute because it appears to be less than 90 degrees.

11. B
$0.25 \times 0.3 \times 400 = 30$

12. D
Back solve by multiplying the two numbers together for each answer choice provided.
$16 \times 18 = 288$

13. A
Of the fractions listed, $\frac{2}{3}$ is closest in value to 0.70.

$$\frac{2}{3} = 0.67$$

$$\frac{4}{7} = 0.57$$

$$\frac{5}{8} = 0.63$$

$$\frac{7}{9} = 0.78$$

14. B
$9(7y + 4) + 7(5y - 1) = -8(y + 4) + 8$
$63y + 36 + 35y - 7 = -8y - 32 + 8$
$98y + 29 = -8y - 24$
$106y = -53$
$y = -\frac{1}{2}$

15. A
A factor divides a number completely without leaving a remainder. 96 has 12 factors: 1, 2, 3, 4, 6, 8, 12, 16, 24, 32, 48, 96

16. A
$$\frac{18x^9}{6x^6} = \frac{18}{6}\left(\frac{x^9}{x^6}\right) = 3x^3$$

17. D
Find the lowest common denominator and convert each fraction. Then identify the smallest number.

$$\frac{2}{5} \times \frac{12}{12} = \frac{24}{60}$$

$$\frac{3}{10} \times \frac{6}{6} = \frac{18}{60}$$

$$\frac{5}{15} \times \frac{4}{4} = \frac{20}{60}$$

$$\frac{4}{20} \times \frac{3}{3} = \frac{12}{60}$$

18. C

$7 - 2(n - q) =$
$7 - 2(n - q) =$
$7 - 2(0) =$
$7 - 0 = 7$

19. D

$(12 - 6y) - (9y - 15) =$
$12 - 6y - 9y + 15 =$
$27 - 15y$

20. B

$y^4 \div 4y + y =$
$4^4 \div (4)(4) + 4 =$
$256 \div 16 + 4 =$
$16 + 4 = 20$

21. C

Because $4^5 = 1,024$, the fifth root of 1,024 is 4.
You could also find the solution by backsolving using the answer choices provided.
$4 \times 4 \times 4 \times 4 \times 4 = 1,024$

22. A

Because ABCD is a square, each side must be of equal length. Therefore AD = DC.
$3x - 1 = 2x + 4$
$x - 1 = 4$
$x = 5$

23. B

$1.5 \times 6^3 =$
$1.5 \times (6 \times 6 \times 6) =$
$1.5 \times 216 = 324$

24. D

$(7 + 3)(6 \div 2)(9 - 4) = (4 + 1)x$
$(10)(3)(5) = 5x$
$(30)(5) = 5x$
$150 = 5x$
$30 = x$

25. A

$3(\sqrt{196} \div \sqrt{49}) =$
$3(14 \div 7) =$
$3(2) = 6$

PRACTICE TEST 3

QUESTIONS

1. If $5x > 310$ and $7x < 483$, which of the following could not be a possible value for x?

   A. 63
   B. 66
   C. 68
   D. 71

2. The cube root of 216 is:

   A. 4
   B. 6
   C. 8
   D. 12

3. If each occurrence of the digit 8 in the number 3,818,298 is replaced with the digit 4, by how much will the number be decreased?

   A. 370,648
   B. 396,482
   C. 404,004
   D. 462,512

4. Convert $\frac{13}{52}$ to a decimal.

   A. 0.15
   B. 0.25
   C. 0.30
   D. 0.35

5. If $5z^2 = 125$, then z can equal which of the following?

   A. +5 or –5
   B. +10 or –10
   C. +15 or –15
   D. +25 or –25

6. What is the sum of all integers from 1 to 250?

   A. 25,840
   B. 28,725
   C. 31,375
   D. 35,950

7. The square root of $(7 + x)^2$ is:

A. $\sqrt{7 + x}$
B. $7 + x$
C. $(7 + x)^3$
D. $(7 + x)^4$

8. If $c - d = 4$, what is the value of $5c - 5d + 5$?

A. 5
B. 15
C. 20
D. 25

9. If $225 \div 5p = n$, what is the value of pn?

A. 45
B. 50
C. 55
D. 60

10. $\sqrt{195}$ is a number between:

A. 5 and 10
B. 10 and 15
C. 15 and 20
D. 20 and 25

11. What type of triangle is XYZ?

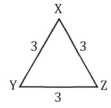

A. Equilateral
B. Obtuse
C. Right
D. Scalene

12. If $t = 3$ and $s = -6$, what is the value of $(tst)(-ts)$?

A. −1,046
B. −984
C. −972
D. −868

13. What is the width of a rectangular box with a volume of 240, a length of 6, and a height of 10?

    A. 3
    B. 4
    C. 5
    D. 6

14. $10^4 \times 10^{-9} \times 10^3 =$

    A. 10^{-108}
    B. 10^{-2}
    C. 10^2
    D. 10^{108}

15. If the average of 4, 9, 12, 15, and y is 10, what is the value of y?

    A. 7
    B. 9
    C. 10
    D. 12

16. Solve for x: $(x - 5)^2 + 16 = (x + 3)^2$

    A. 2
    B. 3
    C. 4
    D. 5

17. The perimeter of a square is 44 inches. What is its area?

    A. 88 square inches
    B. 108 square inches
    C. 112 square inches
    D. 121 square inches

18. In the following diagram, DH = 21, DE = 3, EF = 6, and GH = 3. Solve for FG.

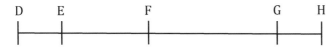

    A. 7
    B. 8
    C. 9
    D. 10

19. Factor $x^2 - 12x + 36$.

    A. $(x - 6)$
    B. $(x + 6)$
    C. $(x - 6)^2$
    D. $(x + 6)^2$

20. $(y^2)^3 - y^2 =$

    A. y^4
    B. $y^6 - y^2$
    C. $y^6 + y^2$
    D. y^{12}

21. If $f = g$, then $34 + 6(f + g) =$

    A. $34 + 12f$
    B. $34 + 12(f + g)$
    C. $40(f + g)$
    D. $40fg$

22. $\sqrt{25} \div \sqrt{49} =$

    A. $\dfrac{5}{9}$
    B. $\dfrac{5}{7}$
    C. 35
    D. 1,225

23. The sum of the measures of the angles of a parallelogram is:

    A. 90 degrees
    B. 180 degrees
    C. 270 degrees
    D. 360 degrees

24. $9\frac{1}{2} - 3\frac{1}{4} - 2\frac{1}{8} =$

    A. $4\frac{1}{4}$
    B. $2\frac{1}{6}$
    C. $4\frac{1}{2}$
    D. $4\frac{1}{8}$

25. Convert 25,700 to scientific notation.

    A. 2.57×10^2
    B. 2.57×10^3
    C. 2.57×10^4
    D. 2.57×10^5

ANSWER KEY

1. D
Step 1: Solve the first equation for x.
$5x > 310$
$x > 62$

Step 2: Solve the second equation for x.
$7x < 483$
$x < 69$

Therefore, x must be between 62 and 69. It cannot be 71.

2. B
Because $6^3 = 216$, the cube root of 216 is 6.
You could also find the solution by backsolving using the answer choices provided.
$6 \times 6 \times 6 = 216$

3. C
$3,818,298 - 3,414,294 = 404,004$

4. B
$\frac{13}{52} = \frac{1}{4} = 0.25$

5. A
$5z^2 = 125$
$z^2 = 25$
$z = +5$ or -5

6. C
To find the sum of a sequence of integers, use the formula $S = \frac{n}{2}(a + b)$, where n is the number of integers, a is the first integer, and b is the last integer.
$S = \frac{250}{2}(1 + 250)$
$S = 125(251)$
$S = 31,375$

7. B
Finding the square root of a number is the inverse operation of squaring that number. Therefore, the square root of $(7 + x)^2$ is $7 + x$.

8. D
Step 1: Solve for c.
$c - d = 4$
$c = 4 + d$

Step 2: Solve the equation by substituting the value of c.
$5c - 5d + 5 =$
$5(4 + d) - 5d + 5 =$
$20 + 5d - 5d + 5 = 25$
$20 + 5 = 25$

9. A

$225 \div 5p = n$

$225 = 5pn$

$45 = pn$

10. B

This problem can be answered through backsolving. If $10^2 = 100$, and $15^2 = 225$, then $\sqrt{195}$ lies between 10 and 15.

11. A

Triangle XYZ is an equilateral triangle because all three sides are equal.

12. C

$(tst)(-ts) =$

$(3 \times -6 \times 3)(-3 \times -6) =$

$-54 \times 18 = -972$

13. B

Volume = length × width × height

$240 = 6 \times$ width $\times 10$

$240 = 60 \times$ width

$4 =$ width

14. B

Add the exponents together because the terms have the same base.

$10^{4+(-9)+3} = 10^{-2}$

15. C

Write the equation as if you're finding the average and then substitute y for the missing number and solve.

$(4 + 9 + 12 + 15 + y) \div 5 = 10$

$(40 + y) \div 5 = 10$

$40 + y = 50$

$y = 10$

16. A

$(x - 5)(x - 5) + 16 = (x + 3)(x + 3)$

$x^2 - 10x + 25 + 16 = x^2 + 6x + 9$

$x^2 - 10x + 41 = x^2 + 6x + 9$

$32 = 16x$

$2 = x$

17. D

Step 1: Find the length of each side. 44 inches $\div 4 = 11$ inches

Step 2: Find the area. 11 inches × 11 inches = 121 square inches

18. C

$21 = DE + EF + FG + GH$

$21 = 3 + 6 + FG + 3$

$21 = 12 + FG$

$9 = FG$

19. C
$x^2 - 12x + 36 =$
$(x - 6)(x - 6) =$
$(x - 6)^2$

20. B
Step 1: $(y^2)^3$ is the same as $(y^2)(y^2)(y^2)$. Because the powers have the same base, they can be multiplied by keeping the base the same and adding the powers together.
$(y^2)(y^2)(y^2) = y^{2+2+2} = y^6$

Step 2: The second (y^2) in the original problem cannot be combined with the first term because they are not like terms. Therefore, the answer is $y^6 - y^2$.

21. A
$34 + 6(f + g) =$
$34 + 6(f + f) =$
$34 + 6(2f) =$
$34 + 12f$

22. B
$\sqrt{25} \div \sqrt{49} =$
$5 \div 7 = \dfrac{5}{7}$

23. D
A parallelogram has four sides, and all four-sided figures have angles that total 360 degrees.

24. D
Convert to the lowest common denominator, which is 12, and then subtract the fractions.
$9\frac{1}{2} - 3\frac{1}{4} - 2\frac{1}{8} =$
$9\frac{4}{8} - 3\frac{2}{8} - 2\frac{1}{8} = 4\frac{1}{8}$

25. C
To convert a number to scientific notation, move the decimal point until there is only one non-zero digit to the left of the decimal point. The resulting decimal number is "a" in Step 1 below. Then count how many places you moved the decimal point. That number is "b" in Step 2 below. If you moved the decimal to the left, then b is positive. If you moved the decimal to the right, then b is negative. The scientific notation number is expressed as "a $\times 10^b$."
Step 1: a = 2.57
Step 2: b = 4
Step 3: 2.57×10^4

PRACTICE TEST 4

QUESTIONS

1. A circle has a radius of 3. What is its area, rounded to the nearest whole number?

    A. 9
    B. 18
    C. 24
    D. 28

2. Which of the following fractions is the largest?

    A. $\dfrac{1}{2}$

    B. $\dfrac{3}{5}$

    C. $\dfrac{4}{6}$

    D. $\dfrac{8}{15}$

3. Solve for x: $(2 \times 2)(6 - 4)(3 + 5) = x^2$

    A. 8
    B. 10
    C. 12
    D. 14

4. The cube of 11 is:

    A. 121
    B. 1,331
    C. 7,421
    D. 14,641

5. $(x^3)^2 + x^3 =$

    A. $x^5 + x^3$
    B. $x^6 + x^3$
    C. x^8
    D. x^9

6. What is the height of a rectangular box with a volume of 375, a width of 5, and a length of 15?

    A. 5
    B. 7
    C. 8
    D. 10

7. If $z = 5$, then $7z \times z =$

    A. 50
    B. 75
    C. 125
    D. 175

8. $(-7)^3 =$

    A. -343
    B. -49
    C. 49
    D. 343

9. Simplify: $3 + 5z + 7 + z - 4 + 2z$

    A. $4 + 4z$
    B. $4 + 6z$
    C. $6 + 8z$
    D. $8 + 6z$

10. If angle Y is 115 degrees, then triangle XYZ is which of the following?

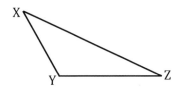

    A. Acute
    B. Equilateral
    C. Obtuse
    D. Right

11. If $0.4y + 1 = 3$, then y equals:

    A. 3
    B. 5
    C. 6
    D. 8

12. Solve: $6!$

    A. 6
    B. 36
    C. 216
    D. 720

13. Simplify $\dfrac{12x^5}{3x^3}$

    A. $4x^2$
    B. $4x^8$
    C. $12x^2$
    D. $12x^8$

14. The product of three consecutive numbers is 1,716. What are the numbers?

    A. 9, 10, 11
    B. 10, 11, 12
    C. 11, 12, 13
    D. 12, 13, 14

15. $10^{-3} \times 10^8 \times 10^2 \times 10^{-5} =$

    A. 10
    B. 100
    C. 1,000
    D. 10,000

16. The degree measures of the three interior angles of a triangle are in the ratio of 1:3:5. What are the measures of the three angles?

    A. 10, 80, 120 degrees
    B. 20, 60, 100 degrees
    C. 30, 40, 110 degrees
    D. 40, 50, 100 degrees

17. $(4x - 6) - (9 - 3x) =$

    A. $1x - 3$
    B. $1x + 3$
    C. $7x - 15$
    D. $7x + 15$

18. If $s + t = 16$ and $s - t = 8$, what is the value of s?

    A. 12
    B. 13
    C. 16
    D. 17

19. $1.584 \times 10^4 =$

    A. 158.4
    B. 1,584
    C. 15,840
    D. 158,400

20. $(9 - 2 \times 2)^2 - 4.5(-6) =$

    A. 43
    B. 45
    C. 49
    D. 52

21. Solve the expression $7c - 5g + 4n$ if $c = -5$, $g = -9$, and $n = 6$.

    A. 31
    B. 34
    C. 36
    D. 40

22. WXYZ is a rectangle with an area of 168. If XY = 12, what is the perimeter?

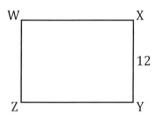

    A. 44
    B. 46
    C. 48
    D. 52

23. Which of the following is a prime number?

    A. 14
    B. 23
    C. 26
    D. 35

24. The fourth root of 81 is:

    A. 3
    B. 4
    C. 6
    D. 9

25. If $y = 7$, what is the value of p in the equation $p = (y^3 + 4) - (7^2 - y)$?

    A. 285
    B. 296
    C. 305
    D. 312

ANSWER KEY

1. D
Area = π × radius^2
Area = 3.14 × 3^2
Area = 3.14 × 9 = 28.26 = 28 (rounded)

2. C
Convert to the lowest common denominator, which is 30, and then identify the largest number.

$$\frac{1}{2} \times \frac{15}{15} = \frac{15}{30}$$

$$\frac{3}{5} \times \frac{6}{6} = \frac{18}{30}$$

$$\frac{4}{6} \times \frac{5}{5} = \frac{20}{30}$$

$$\frac{8}{15} \times \frac{2}{2} = \frac{16}{30}$$

3. A
$(2 \times 2)(6 - 4)(3 + 5) = x^2$
$(4)(2)(8) = x^2$
$64 = x^2$
$8 = x$

4. B
The cube of 11 is 11^3, which is 11 × 11 × 11 = 1,331

5. B
Step 1: $(x^3)^2$ is the same as $(x^3)(x^3)$. Because the powers have the same base, they can be multiplied by keeping the base the same and adding the powers together.
$(x^3)(x^3) = x^{3+3} = x^6$

Step 2: The second (x^3) of the original problem cannot be combined with the first term because they are not like terms. Therefore, the answer is $x^6 + x^3$.

6. A
Volume = length × width × height
375 = 15 × 5 × height
375 = 75 × height
5 = height

7. D
$7z \times z =$
$7(5) \times 5 =$
$35 \times 5 = 175$

8. A
$(-7)^3 =$
$(-7)(-7)(-7) = -343$

9. C
$3 + 5z + 7 + z - 4 + 2z =$
$6 + 8z$

10. C
Triangle XYZ is an obtuse triangle because it has one obtuse angle (greater than 90 degrees) and two acute angles.

11. B
$0.4y + 1 = 3$
$0.4y = 2$
$y = 2 \div 0.4 = 5$

12. D
The factorial (!) is the product of an integer and all the integers below it, down to 1.
$6! = 6 \times 5 \times 4 \times 3 \times 2 \times 1 = 720$

13. A
$$\frac{12x^5}{3x^3} = \frac{12}{3}\left(\frac{x^5}{x^3}\right) = 4x^2$$

14. C
Back solve by multiplying the three numbers together for each answer choice provided.
$11 \times 12 \times 13 = 1{,}716$

15. B
Add the exponents together because the terms have the same base, then solve.
$10^{-3+8+2+(-5)} = 10^2$
$10^2 = 100$

16. B
Because the three interior angles of a triangle must equal 180 degrees, the measures of the angles can be determined through the following equation: $1x + 3x + 5x = 180$

Step 1: Solve for x.
$1x + 3x + 5x = 180$
$9x = 180$
$x = 20$

Step 2: Calculate the measure of each angle.
$1x = 1(20) = 20$
$3x = 3(20) = 60$
$5x = 5(20) = 100$
The measures of the three angles are 20, 60, and 100 degrees.

17. C
$(4x - 6) - (9 - 3x) =$
$4x - 6 - 9 + 3x =$
$7x - 15$

18. A
Step 1: Solve the first equation for t.
$s + t = 16$
$t = 16 - s$

Step 2: Solve the second equation for s by substituting the known value of t from step 1.
$s - t = 8$
$s - (16 - s) = 8$
$s - 16 + s = 8$
$2s = 24$
$s = 12$

19. C
$1.584 \times 10^4 =$
$1.584 \times 10 \times 10 \times 10 \times 10 =$
$1.584 \times 10,000 = 15,840$
Alternatively, you could move the decimal point four places to the right because 10 is raised to the fourth power. Therefore 1.584 becomes 15,840.

20. D
$(9 - 2 \times 2)^2 - 4.5(-6) =$
$(9 - 4)^2 - 4.5(-6) =$
$5^2 - 4.5(-6) =$
$25 - 4.5(-6) =$
$25 + 27 = 52$

21. B
$7c - 5g + 4n =$
$7(-5) - 5(-9) + 4(6) =$
$-35 + 45 + 24 = 34$

22. D
Because WXYZ is a rectangle, $XY = WZ$ and $WX = ZY$.

Step 1: Solve for ZY by using the formula for the area of a rectangle.
Area $=$ length $\times$ width
$168 = ZY \times 12$
$14 = ZY$

Step 2: Find the perimeter by adding the four sides together: $12 + 12 + 14 + 14 = 52$

23. B
A prime number is a whole number greater than 1 whose only factors are 1 and the number itself. The only prime number listed is 23.

24. A
Because $3^4 = 81$, the fourth root of 81 is 3.
You could also find the solution by backsolving using the answer choices provided.
$3 \times 3 \times 3 \times 3 = 81$

25. C

$p = (y^3 + 4) - (7^2 - y)$

$p = (7^3 + 4) - (7^2 - 7)$

$p = (343 + 4) - (49 - 7)$

$p = 347 - 42 = 305$

PRACTICE TEST 5

QUESTIONS

1. If a circle has a radius of 9, what is its circumference rounded to the nearest whole number?

   A. 28
   B. 36
   C. 57
   D. 81

2. The reciprocal of $\frac{1}{5}$ is:

   A. $\frac{1}{25}$
   B. $\frac{1}{5}$
   C. 5
   D. 25

3. If $6 + n = m - 4$, then $m - n =$

   A. 5
   B. 8
   C. 9
   D. 10

4. $x^2 \times x^6 =$

   A. x^4
   B. x^8
   C. x^{12}
   D. x^{64}

5. If $0.20 \div x = 1$, then $x =$

   A. 0.2
   B. 0.4
   C. 1
   D. 2

6. Solve the following inequality: $\frac{1}{2}(4x - 6) + 8 > 4x + 1$

   A. $1 > x$
   B. $2 > x$
   C. $2 < x$
   D. $3 < x$

7. Angles A and B are:

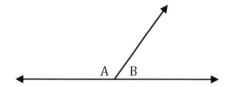

   A. Complementary angles
   B. Reflex angles
   C. Right angles
   D. Supplementary angles

8. $(812 + 331 - 431 + 102) \div 2 =$

   A. 398
   B. 401
   C. 407
   D. 415

9. What is the perimeter of a right triangle with perpendicular sides of 3 inches and 4 inches?

   A. 7 inches
   B. 12 inches
   C. 18 inches
   D. 25 inches

10. 32% can be converted to which of the following fractions?

   A. $\dfrac{4}{18}$
   B. $\dfrac{6}{20}$
   C. $\dfrac{8}{25}$
   D. $\dfrac{9}{36}$

11. In the graph $4x + 2y = 12$, at what point is the y-axis intersected?

   A. $(0, 6)$
   B. $(0, 3)$
   C. $(3, 0)$
   D. $(6, 0)$

12. In which of the following numbers is the sum of the digits equal to the product of the digits?

    A. 1,193
    B. 1,248
    C. 1,376
    D. 1,412

13. Which of the following is closest in value to the decimal 0.40?

    A. $\dfrac{2}{6}$

    B. $\dfrac{2}{7}$

    C. $\dfrac{3}{8}$

    D. $\dfrac{4}{9}$

14. What is the sum of all integers from 1 to 670?

    A. 218,630
    B. 224,785
    C. 231,472
    D. 245,491

15. If $\dfrac{c}{4} = 20$, then $\dfrac{c}{10} =$

    A. 8
    B. 10
    C. 11
    D. 15

16. What type of triangle is XYZ?

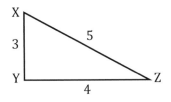

    A. Equilateral
    B. Isosceles
    C. Obtuse
    D. Scalene

17. What is the prime factorization of 88?

    A. $2^2 \times 11$
    B. $2^3 \times 7$
    C. $2^3 \times 11$
    D. $2^4 \times 8$

18. If the perimeter of a rectangle is 50 inches, and one side has a length of 10 inches, then what is its area, in square inches?

    A. 120 square inches
    B. 140 square inches
    C. 150 square inches
    D. 180 square inches

19. If $x = 3$, then $x^x(x^x) =$

    A. 81
    B. 243
    C. 486
    D. 729

20. $\sqrt{-81}$ is an example of which of the following?

    A. Imaginary number
    B. Negative number
    C. Real number
    D. Whole number

21. Convert 0.0036 to scientific notation.

    A. 3.6×10^{-4}
    B. 3.6×10^{-3}
    C. 3.6×10^3
    D. 3.6×10^4

22. The square root of $(8 - y)^2$ is:

    A. $\sqrt{8 - y}$
    B. $8 - y$
    C. $(8 - y)^2$
    D. $(8 - y)^4$

23. In the number 62.37, which digit is in the hundredths place?

   A. 6
   B. 2
   C. 3
   D. 7

24. A square box has 11-inch sides. What is its volume?

   A. 121 cubic inches
   B. 726 cubic inches
   C. 1,331 cubic inches
   D. 14,641 cubic inches

25. 65% of 10% of 800 is:

   A. 52
   B. 68
   C. 76
   D. 89

ANSWER KEY

1. C
Circumference $= 2 \times \pi \times$ radius
Circumference $= 2 \times 3.14 \times 9 = 56.52 = 57$ (rounded)

2. C
The reciprocal of a number can be found by interchanging its numerator and denominator. Therefore, the reciprocal of $\frac{1}{5}$ is $\frac{5}{1}$, which can be rewritten as 5.

3. D
$6 + n = m - 4$
$6 = m - n - 4$
$10 = m - n$

4. B
Because the powers have the same base, they can be multiplied by keeping the base the same and adding the powers together. $x^2 \times x^6 = x^{2+6} = x^8$

5. A
$0.20 \div x = 1$
$x = 1 \times 0.2 = 0.2$

6. B
$\frac{1}{2}(4x - 6) + 8 > 4x + 1$
$2x - 3 + 8 > 4x + 1$
$2x + 5 > 4x + 1$
$5 > 2x + 1$
$4 > 2x$
$2 > x$

7. D
Supplementary angles are two angles whose measures add up to 180 degrees. Supplementary angles, when placed adjacent to each other, form a straight line or 180 degree angle, as demonstrated in the diagram.

8. C
$(812 + 331 - 431 + 102) \div 2 =$
$(814) \div 2 = 407$

9. B
Step 1: Find the length of the hypotenuse by using the Pythagorean theorem.
$a^2 + b^2 = c^2$
$(3)^2 + (4)^2 = c^2$
$9 + 16 = c^2$
$25 = c^2$
$5 = c$

Step 2: Add the length of the three sides to find the perimeter of the triangle.
3 inches + 4 inches + 5 inches = 12 inches

10. C

32% can be rewritten as $\frac{32}{100}$. This fraction can be reduced to $\frac{8}{25}$ by dividing the numerator and denominator by 4.

11. A

$4x + 2y = 12$ is the equation for a line. To find the point where the line intersects the y-axis, let $x = 0$ and solve the equation.

$4x + 2y = 12$
$4(0) + 2y = 12$
$2y = 12$
$y = 6$

The line intersects the y-axis at $(0, 6)$.

12. D

Back solve by adding and then multiplying each digit for the answer choices provided.
$1 + 4 + 1 + 2 = 8$
$1 \times 4 \times 1 \times 2 = 8$
The answer is 1,412.

13. C

Of the fractions listed, $\frac{3}{8}$ is closest in value to 0.40.
$\frac{2}{6} = 0.33$

$\frac{2}{7} = 0.29$

$\frac{3}{8} = 0.38$

$\frac{4}{9} = 0.44$

14. B

To find the sum of a sequence of integers, use the formula $S = \frac{n}{2}(a + b)$, where n is the number of integers, a is the first integer, and b is the last integer.
$S = \frac{670}{2}(1 + 670)$
$S = 335(671)$
$S = 224{,}785$

15. A

Step 1: Solve for c.
$\frac{c}{4} = 20$
$c = 20 \times 4 = 80$

Step 2: Solve the equation by substituting the value of c.
$\frac{c}{10} = \frac{80}{10} = 8$

16. D
Triangle XYZ is a scalene triangle because each side has a different length.

17. C
$88 =$
$44 \times 2 =$
$22 \times 2 \times 2 =$
$11 \times 2 \times 2 \times 2 =$
$2^3 \times 11$

18. C
Step 1: Calculate the width of the rectangle by using the perimeter formula.
Perimeter $= (2 \times \text{length}) + (2 \times \text{width})$
50 inches $= (2 \times 10 \text{ inches}) + (2 \times \text{width})$
50 inches $= 20 \text{ inches} + (2 \times \text{width})$
50 inches – 20 inches $= 2 \times \text{width}$
30 inches $= 2 \times \text{width}$
15 inches $= \text{width}$

Step 2: Calculate the area of the rectangle.
Area $= \text{length} \times \text{width}$
Area $= 10 \text{ inches} \times 15 \text{ inches} = 150$ square inches

19. D
$x^x(x^x) =$
$3^3(3^3) =$
$27 \times 27 = 729$

20. A
$\sqrt{-81}$ is an imaginary number because the square root of a negative number doesn't exist.

21. B
To convert a number to scientific notation, move the decimal point until there is only one non-zero digit to the left of the decimal point. The resulting decimal number is "a" in Step 1 below. Then count how many places you moved the decimal point. That number is "b" in Step 2 below. If you moved the decimal to the left, then b is positive. If you moved the decimal to the right, then b is negative. The scientific notation number is expressed as "a $\times 10^b$."
Step 1: $a = 3.6$
Step 2: $b = -3$
Step 3: 3.6×10^{-3}

22. B
Finding the square root of a number is the inverse operation of squaring that number. Therefore, the square root of $(8 - y)^2$ is $8 - y$.

23. D
6 is in the tens place
2 is in the ones place
3 is in the tenths place
7 is in the hundredths place.

24. C
Volume = length × width × height
Volume = 11 inches × 11 inches × 11 inches = 1,331 cubic inches

25. A
$0.65 \times 0.1 \times 800 =$
$0.65 \times 80 = 52$

PRACTICE TEST 6

QUESTIONS

1. If 9 − d = 17 + p, then p + d =

    A. −26
    B. −8
    C. 7
    D. 8

2. A square box has a volume of 216 cubic inches. What is the perimeter of one of its faces?

    A. 16 inches
    B. 18 inches
    C. 20 inches
    D. 24 inches

3. (8 − 3)! =

    A. 106
    B. 112
    C. 120
    D. 132

4. If x = 2, then $(x^x)(x^x) \div (x^x) + x =$

    A. 6
    B. 8
    C. 12
    D. 18

5. $(18 − 10 \div 2)^2 − 3.25(−4) =$

    A. 163
    B. 171
    C. 182
    D. 197

6. If 0.25x = 1, then x equals:

    A. 2
    B. 4
    C. 8
    D. 10

7. In the following figure, if angle Z is an acute angle, then angle Y can measure which of the following?

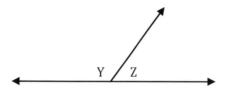

A. 70 degrees
B. 75 degrees
C. 85 degrees
D. 115 degrees

8. Given the equation $\dfrac{z + 4c}{b + c} = 8$, what is z in terms of b and c?

A. $z = 4b + 4c$
B. $z = 8b + 4c$
C. $z = 8b + 8c$
D. $z = 12b + 8c$

9. Simplify $\sqrt{144y^2}$

A. $12y$
B. $12y^2$
C. $144y$
D. $144y^2$

10. If $x + z = 9$ and $x - z = 5$, what is the value of x?

A. 4
B. 6
C. 7
D. 9

11. The number 0.54 is what percent of 96?

A. 0.05625%
B. 0.5625%
C. 5.625%
D. 56.25%

12. Which of the following can be rewritten as the product of 4 and y is equal to 5 less than z?

    A. $4y = z - 5$
    B. $4y = z + 5$
    C. $4 = 5 + z$
    D. $4 \div 7 = z - 5$

13. $7.5 \times 10^2 =$

    A. 75
    B. 750
    C. 7,500
    D. 75,000

14. Solve the expression $18a - 24b + 13c - 9d$ if $a = -2$, $b = -4$, $c = 7$, and $d = 9$.

    A. 53
    B. 59
    C. 66
    D. 70

15. 40% can be converted to which of the following fractions?

    A. $\dfrac{6}{16}$
    B. $\dfrac{8}{18}$
    C. $\dfrac{8}{20}$
    D. $\dfrac{6}{24}$

16. If a triangle has a base of 6 and a height of 10, what is its area?

    A. 8
    B. 30
    C. 45
    D. 60

17. How many factors does the number 42 have?

    A. 6
    B. 7
    C. 8
    D. 9

18. Factor $x^2 - 8x + 16$.

    A. $(x - 4)^2$
    B. $(x + 4)^2$
    C. $(x + 4)(x - 2)$
    D. $(x + 4)(x + 2)$

19. Which of the following is the sum of the interior angles of rectangle WXYZ?

    A. 90 degrees
    B. 180 degrees
    C. 270 degrees
    D. 360 degrees

20. Which of the following is a prime number?

    A. 69
    B. 71
    C. 77
    D. 87

21. In which of the following numbers is the sum of the cube of each of the digits equal to the number itself?

    A. 114
    B. 127
    C. 153
    D. 186

22. If $z = \dfrac{1}{4}$, what is the value of y when $\dfrac{5}{z} = \dfrac{y}{8}$?

    A. 160
    B. 172
    C. 185
    D. 190

23. If $x = 3$, then $x^3 \div x =$

    A. 9
    B. 27
    C. 54
    D. 81

24. A square box has 19-inch sides. What is its volume?

    A. 361 cubic inches
    B. 3,430 cubic inches
    C. 5,144 cubic inches
    D. 6,859 cubic inches

25. If $m = 4$, then $m(m) \times m =$

    A. 16
    B. 32
    C. 64
    D. 128

ANSWER KEY

1. B
$9 - d = 17 + p$
$9 - 17 = p + d$
$-8 = p + d$

2. D
Step 1: Volume = length × width × height. Because the box is square, the length, width, and height must be the same. Therefore, you must find the cube root of 216, which is 6.

Step 2: If one of the sides is 6 inches, and the box is square, then all four sides of the face must be 6 inches. The perimeter of one of the faces is 6 inches × 4 = 24 inches.

3. C
The factorial (!) is the product of an integer and all the integers below it, down to 1.
$(8 - 3)! = 5! = 5 \times 4 \times 3 \times 2 \times 1 = 120$

4. A
$(x^x)(x^x) \div (x^x) + x =$
$(2^2)(2^2) \div (2^2) + 2 =$
$(4)(4) \div 4 + 2 =$
$16 \div 4 + 2 =$
$4 + 2 = 6$

5. C
$(18 - 10 \div 2)^2 - 3.25(-4) =$
$(18 - 5)^2 - 3.25(-4) =$
$13^2 - 3.25(-4) =$
$169 - 3.25(-4) =$
$169 + 13 = 182$

6. B
$0.25x = 1$
$x = 1 \div 0.25$
$x = 4$

7. D
If angle Z is an acute angle, then it must be between 0 and 90 degrees. Because the sum of supplementary angles must equal 180 degrees, angle Y must therefore be greater than 90 degrees. Of the answer choices provided, the only possible answer is 115 degrees.

8. B
Step 1: Multiply each side of the equation by b + c.
$z + 4c = 8(b + c)$

Step 2: Simplify the equation to solve for z.
$z + 4c = 8(b + c)$
$z + 4c = 8b + 8c$
$z = 8b + 8c - 4c$
$z = 8b + 4c$

9. A

Be careful not to mistake $\sqrt{144y^2}$ for $(\sqrt{144y})^2$. $144y^2$ can be rewritten as $(12y)^2$. Finding the square root of a number is the inverse operation of squaring that number. Therefore, the square root of $(12y)^2$ is $12y$.

10. C

Step 1: Solve the first equation for z.
$x + z = 9$
$z = 9 - x$

Step 2: Solve the second equation for x by substituting the known value of z from step 1.
$x - z = 5$
$x - (9 - x) = 5$
$x - 9 + x = 5$
$2x = 14$
$x = 7$

11. B

$0.54 \div 96 = 0.005625 = 0.5625\%$

12. A

The product of 4 and y is equal to 5 less than z can be rewritten as $4y = z - 5$.

13. B

$7.5 \times 10^2 =$
$7.5 \times 10 \times 10 =$
$7.5 \times 100 = 750$

14. D

$18a - 24b + 13c - 9d =$
$18(-2) - 24(-4) + 13(7) - 9(9) =$
$-36 + 96 + 91 - 81 = 70$

15. C

40% can be rewritten as $\frac{40}{100}$. This fraction can be reduced to $\frac{8}{20}$ by dividing the numerator and denominator by 5.

16. B

Area = ½ base × height
Area = $0.5 \times 6 \times 10 = 30$

17. C

A factor divides a number completely without leaving a remainder. 42 has 8 factors: 1, 2, 3, 6, 7, 14, 21, 42

18. A

$x^2 - 8x + 16 =$
$(x - 4)(x - 4) =$
$(x - 4)^2$

19. D

Because the rectangle contains four right angles, and each right angle measures 90 degrees, the interior angles total 360 degrees. Also, the rectangle has four sides, and all four-sided figures have angles that total 360 degrees.

20. B

A prime number is a whole number greater than 1 whose only factors are 1 and the number itself. The only prime number listed is 71.

21. C

Back solve by cubing each digit and then adding the numbers together for each answer choice provided.

$1^3 + 5^3 + 3^3 =$
$(1 \times 1 \times 1) + (5 \times 5 \times 5) + (3 \times 3 \times 3) =$
$1 + 125 + 27 = 153$

22. A

Step 1: Convert $\frac{1}{4}$ to a decimal and substitute for z.

$$\frac{5}{0.25} = \frac{y}{8}$$

Step 2: Cross multiply and solve for y.
$5 \times 8 = 0.25y$
$40 = 0.25y$
$160 = y$

23. A

$x^3 \div x =$
$3^3 \div 3 =$
$27 \div 3 = 9$

24. D

Volume = length × width × height
Volume = 19 inches × 19 inches × 19 inches = 6,859 cubic inches

25. C

$m(m) \times m =$
$4(4) \times 4 =$
$16 \times 4 = 64$

Made in the USA
Columbia, SC
06 January 2021